Tide-

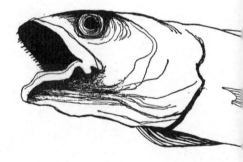

Also in the Seren Classics series

Tide-race

Brenda Chamberlain

With drawings by the Author

Afterword by Jonah Jones

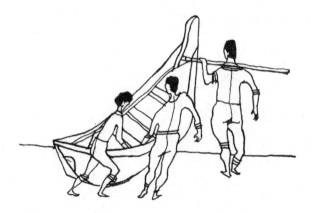

SEREN BOOKS

seren is the book imprint of
Poetry Wales Press Ltd.
57 Nolton Street, Bridgend, Wales, CF31 3AE
www.seren-books.com

ISBN-10: 0-907476-65-1
ISBN-13: 978-0-907476-65-8

A CIP record for this title is available from the British Library.

The publisher acknowledges the financial assistance of the Welsh Books Council.

Cover painting : 'Seascape in Red' by Brenda Chamberlain

Printed by Bell & Bain Ltd, Glasgow

TO
My Neighbours
On The Island

CONTENTS

You Who Are In The Traffic Of The
World: Can You Guess The Thoughts Of
An Islander?

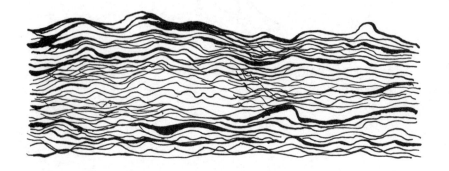

THE ISLANDERS

AT PANT, a double-house
Cadwaladr Tomos (the Bull-neck). Postman, farmer,
boatman, boatbuilder
Nans, his wife
Owain, Myfanwy, Tudur, Siani, their children

AT CLOGWYN, a double-house
Twm Huws, Pantannas (Twm Clogwyn) sometimes
known as Pantannas from the farm where he was born
on the mainland: most often, as Twm Clogwyn from
the name of his island farm. Fisherman and boatbuilder
Sarah, his wife
Samson, their son
Dai Penmon, natural son of Sarah Huws, called her
nephew
The King, great-uncle to Sarah

AT CLOGWYN BACH
Dic Jones, the Longshanks, natural brother to Jacob Lloyd
Leah, his wife
Their four young children and baby, Ianto

AT TY DRAW, a double-house
Jacob Lloyd, lobster-fisher and farmer
Rhiannon, his wife, sister to Leah
Eira, their daughter

AT PEN CRAIG, THEN AT GARTHWEN
Stewart Hopkinson
Alice, his wife

AT TY BYCHAN, THEN AT PEN CRAIG
Paul and the author

AT PEN CRAIG, THEN AT GARTHWEN
Bill Levens
Zöe Levens, his wife
Harold, Douglas, Vera, their children

AT GARTHWEN
Wolfgang, the Polish hermit

AT THE LIGHTHOUSE
Merfyn Edwards, assistant lighthouse-keeper, and two
others

AT TY DRAW ISAF
Jack Isaacson, called the Ancient Mariner
His wife
Their children

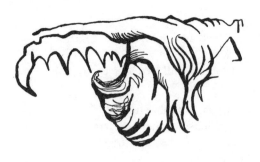

FOREWORD

From the end of the peninsula, the island which has been my home for fourteen years, wears an austere aspect. On the eastward side the mountain drops sheer to the sea. The kindly westward side with its scattered farmhouses is not visible from here. Between mainland and sea-rock run the inconstant waters of the Sound. It is the end of our world.

Paul and I came to live here in the spring of 1947. In those days it was easy to rent houses on the island. Several were in disrepair and had not been lived in for years. At first sight, the architecture of the eighty-year-old farmhouse was a disappointment and a surprise. I had expected something more romantic, a crofter's cottage on the strand; fishing nets before the door, in keeping with the extreme simplicity of the limited landscape. Now that I live here, in a four-square granite house that no winds can shake, I feel differently. It is good to have a little distance between the house and the sea; even so, on winter nights the roaring of the surf is monstrous. It booms as if under the foundations. There is no escape from the raving of wind and water.

A house on an island is not quite like other homes; one feels impossibly far when away from it; and when there, it is sometimes a prison, and sometimes a sanctuary. It has its own calm atmosphere, something to do with the silent and remote island air; but perhaps it has more to do with the fact that the house is built from the ruins of the sixth-century abbey. The roof is cleverly broken up and there are no eaves. The south-wester simply streams over it; there is no plucking at the slates as there was in the cottage in the mountains where I lived during the war.

There are no dark corners. At breakfast-time, the living-room is bright with the sun shining over the mountain; and supper-time on a summer evening in the little study facing west across the Irish Sea to the horns of the Wicklows, is a time of molten gold and flame-coloured water, and of a beneficent peace. The living-room has a fireplace which is a joy to use. It was made a few years ago, out of old bricks from a pulled-down chimney. The wood fire is laid on an iron basket which, being high up, throws out a good heat. The iron oven beside it is large enough to accommodate a goose and a week's baking of bread. The oven is stoked by a separate fire underneath: it has an excellent draught, and is economical of wood.

The house has eight rooms; a dairy, kitchen, children's room, study; and four bedrooms, one of which I use as a studio. Upstairs, there is a wide landing lit by a skylight.

At the north side of the house is a small walled garden. The well is only a few yards away from the door; the outlet stream is completely hidden by watercress. We are seldom at a loss for salad; lettuce, watercress, and dandelion in the early spring.

We have no electricity. For lighting, we use paraffin lamps and candles; for heating, wood fires and a paraffin radiator. We have no need of coal since driftwood is easily obtainable; and at times one can find quantities of paraffin wax washed up by the tide. The wax we mould into candles which are then threaded with fishing line for wicks; and the result gives out a quite special kind of radiance, a votive flame.

We are a small community, only about twelve now, interdependent but at the same time independent. Our neighbours are fisher-farmers with feet on the earth and hands in the sea. To a great extent, we live off the fruits of our environment: lobster, crab, crayfish, mackerel and pollack in the summer, and rockfish caught from the rocks in calm weather the whole year round.

Life on this, as on every small island, is controlled by the moods of the sea; its tides, its gifts, its deprivations.

ONE

THE CAVE OF SEALS

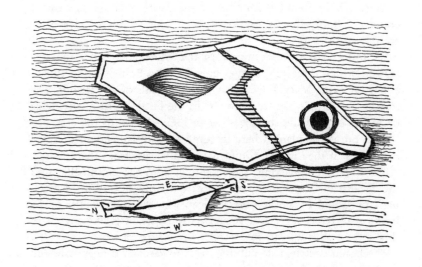

Here I am, here I am, wrested, reeling.
Can I dare? Can I plunge?

R. M. Rilke

I

LISTEN: I have found the home of my heart. I could not eat: I could not think straight any more; so I came to this solitary place and lay in the sun.

Six miles across the Sound from the white village lies the sea-crag to which three pilgrimages equal one to Rome. At the ruined abbey of Saint Mary I will pray for the souls of my friends. The treasures of Britain are to be found in the fertile earth of the fields or in the bays of the southwest or in the seal-cave to the east; for Merlin buried or planted here in some secret place certain mystical properties. If they can be found, you shall learn from them.

The question was, could I dare plunge into the hermit-life, into the fisherman-farmer's? Alone; most certainly not. With a man, perhaps. Could I take the outward leap into the great depths of the living sea? I was eager and yet mortally afraid of giving myself to this sort of adventurous Robinson Crusoe-type of existence.

The beach stretched its curving arms towards two green islets in the bay, with the inhabited island away to the westward out of sight. The sands were poor and colourless; there were no splendid cliffs, no fishermen to be seen, no craft on the water.

Walking up and down at the tide-edge, Friedrich offered me a drink from a silver flask, and asked:

'Do you not find this place full of atmosphere?'

Behind us at the top of the strand rose a strong wall to keep back the sea from the graveyard and the grey church with its twin transepts. The headstones standing erect on the rising ground were like so many birds on nesting ledges.

There was no sign of a boat coming for us. Friedrich began to grow anxious, because it was already long past the time at which he had been told to be on the beach.

'Perhaps,' said Friedrich unhappily; 'Perhaps a cow has calved or the boatman is ill.'

A black dot appeared off the furthest headland, and soon we were able to make out a motor boat close-in under the land.

They were coming for us!

There were two men in the boat: from their appearance, they might have been father and son. Nodding briefly to us, they began to remove boxes of lobsters from the scuppers of the boat, and walked away towards the village.

A little later, the elder of the two, a short man in thigh waders, carried us in turn, like sacks from the sand of the steeply-shelving beach into the motor boat.

Ah, chapel by the sea, with blue and white headstones erect as birds on nesting ledges; white of razorbills' breasts, blue of black-backed gulls, I was leaving you and the mainland traffic and highways; with its green and yellow gilded trees, the hyacinth-carpeted undergrowth, the fine-drawn shoulders of mountains withdrawn from primitive foothills.

The sea was almost dead calm, a summer calm already in May. The inner side of an oyster shell, or silk shaken out in shallow folds.

Over the face of the elder man whose name we discovered was Twm Huws Pantannas, reflections from the oyster-blue waves ran clear with light, and the bronze of his skin proclaimed him fisherman-farmer. He had a suave, untroubled, crafty face; and a sort of radiance lent by the sun striking sparks from the sea, streamed from him. His face was covered with a fine trellis-work of wrinkles, and there was a fox-cunning smile about his mouth; but the brightness of the day and the glamour of the salt air gave to him a deceptive calm amd simplicity.

The suave, secretive faces of sea-farers! You may know them by the radiance that streams from their cheeks and brows. Their lips are cunning as they smile with mouths of men who have almost mastered fear.

The sea took us, and it became immaterial whether we made landfall or not. We began to live in the present moment and, Miracle! time did stand still on the waters between here and there.

The inhospitable island had seduced mystics since the sixth century. There is less wonder in the number of men buried in its earth than in the enigma of why it first became a magnet to the long-thighed ones travelling the sacred roads following the sun towards the west. And ·the inhabitants have been free since the earliest times from nearly all diseases, and live to extreme old age.

The finger of the Stone Mother points to it, and it is in the far west, but this cold hill descending into the sea has gulfs about her sides, through which grinning dogfish move in twenty fathoms of water. So old are her enchantments, so subtle, that we who cling to the vestiges of the legendary past, sink unknowingly into the moulds of our race, becoming upon her shores Mankind in search of a sign from heaven.

Who can distinguish between the dust of the saint and the lecher?

Like bell-sounds, their spoken names: Lleuddad, Dafydd, Deiniol, Beuno, Dyfrig Beneurog.

Birds flew low over the surface of the dreaming waves.

There were five of us aboard; the two islanders, Twm Huws and Dai Penmon, Friedrich and me, and the man who had followed us down the beach, the vagabond Ancient Mariner. He was an Englishman, his face weathered by sea and wind; and he wore clothes so shapeless and stained that he might have been a shipwrecked sailor just rescued from a coral island; but judging from the familiar way in which he lounged in the stern I guessed that he too was an inhabitant of the island. The young man Dai Penmon stood at the tiller, his face inscrutable.

Our boat softly breasted an indigo, green, and violet sea; we were rocked absurdly like toys, up and down, momentarily fixed, as if the event of being brought together held enough significance to make time stand still.

Clear as glass in the blue and gold day the rock Leviathan lying to the westward sent out an unending cry.

The islets to the south, the sheltered coves fell away from us. The headland was splashed with flowers over which gulls stood preening their feathers.

The cockle-shell in which we sat began to nose its way through the treacherous currents of the Sound. Friedrich sat beside me, his kindly round face at peace, his mind far away in romantic dreams. In the stern the three men were gossiping about dogs, cattle and sheep.

Friedrich broke his reverie to ask Twm if there would be accommodation for us when we landed. With obvious malice, Twm answered: 'No, nothing, but there are plenty of empty houses.'

Friedrich was horrified.

'But it was all arranged months ago,' he stammered. 'The postmaster arranged everything; the boat, the house where we were to stay, everything.'

Twm continued to smile, and to repeat that there were plenty of empty houses.

The land fell away; the world became two elements, water and air. The cockle-shell in which we sat, how brave and gay it was, nosing for home through the Sound.

From the sea, the hump of rock looked idyllic, a place of pilgrimage to the neophyte. It was so calm that we seemed not to be moving; it was the island that swung slowly round to meet us out of the blue ocean. On her eastward side her five hundred foot mountain stood sheer behind salty vapours that gave her an austerity, an aloofness.

The Ancient Mariner glared forth, one eye focused, the other unfixed as if he saw either nothing or everything too blindingly.

Twm seemed possessed of an ancient virility in the strong thrust of his thighs, and in his smile that told nothing. Fisherman, farmer, boatbuilder, he was probably of all those living at that time on the island, the most close in spirit to the original islanders who some twenty years before, had become disgusted at the invasion of the mainlanders, and had left their homes and gone forth to live on the peninsula.

Friedrich sat unmoving, lost in visions of the past. O let the past sleep on. The bones of the faithful make for a fertile earth. The past is too much with us.

Those lamenting sea-birds are the present, the wings of the bright today. The sea is too salt, too alive to admit of ghosts. Friedrich can see them though: processions of saints lighting beacon fires in the cave near the sacred well; beacons speaking a fire-code: 'We have come, we are holy men and seers. Put out your boats for us.'

In his mind he was watching an answering flame rise up from the brow of the island. A watcher in the rocks, a forerunner of Twm, another man with a twist in his soul, could see the pilgrims' pyre, but would send out no answering signal; instead, he quietly retreated down the mountain, feeling a kingliness in his blood at the thought of his power over men, a power that lay in voluntary isolation. He drew power to himself and thought, 'On the third day after tomorrow (if it is clear weather) I shall suddenly appear to them on the waves majestically, a sea creature battling with the current in open combat.'

Maen Bugail, in her blackness and savagery resembling a wrecked coaster, lay in the distance of the Sound. She is full in the track of the tide which, forking at Pen Dinmor the south-easternmost tip of the island, runs north-westward, and setting round the north headland, runs between her and the sea-rock. The other tongue of the tide sets outside Craig y Llanw to meet the first stream over a mile from the island. From their mingling, a convulsion of water sets back against the sides of the island.

We passed close under black and lichen-encrusted cliffs; nearer, nearer, close, close, until the fangs of wet rock were snapping at us; but in this proximity there was safety, for we were in slack water, in a sullen backwash. Rock rose in galleries and on every shelf stood solemn congregations of sea-birds. We slowly crept past the ramparts of this world of birds.

And still there was no sign of any place where a man might build himself a shelter.

At last, the high land fell away and we were in the anchorage.

Seated four-square on the middle of the beach was an ancient man with a neptune beard and flowing hair. He had a light metal crown chased with a design of seahorses and shells, worn slightly sideways on his head, and in his crablike fingers he held a plug of twist from which he was cutting thin wafers of tobacco. By his side lay an empty rum bottle. He was gross with majesty, and must have been a good trencherman and an heroic drinker. He reeked of fish and salt and tarry ropes.

Behind the old King lay the boats with one many times bigger than the rest; a great black cattle-boat nearly a hundred years old, of giant proportions. She looked as if she had been built for the use of trolls, but the planks of her bottom were now broken and weakened from the lashing of hoofs and the weight of furniture, for she had been in constant use for carrying stock and possessions to and from the island.

Twm said, 'You might try at each farm for a lodging. It's no use asking at our house. We are full up. There are plenty of empty houses.'

Empty houses. We were by now very hungry, and had no food with us; no blankets, no tents.

We followed the cart track that ran from the lighthouse in the south to the abbey ruins in the north. Before us lay the western side; sweet-smelling, level, and fertile. We turned in at the first farm and asked a dark-haired woman with a pouter-pigeon breast whether she could provide us with food and shelter. From the open doorway came a smell of freshly baked bread and cakes.

'No,' said the woman, 'I cannot take you in. My house is full of children.'

'No,' said the stout blonde woman barring the door of the second house. 'There's no room here.'

She was openly hostile.

The third house was empty, dark, and locked.

The fourth house lay away from the path at the bottom of a steep field. A thread of smoke was rising from its chimneys. Out in the meadow, a foxy-looking dog barked at us, and a tall man came out, but quickly went inside again.

I knocked at the door. A Scots voice called:

'Come in.'

A thin man was standing in the middle of the room, staring at us in amazement. On a table in the window was a loaf of bread, a half bottle of whisky and an empty tumbler.

The man hesitated, searching for words. At last he said:

'Come in, make yourselves at home.' He added: 'My wife is away on the mainland,' as he cleared chairs for us.

'You see,' he went on to explain, 'This isn't my house. It belongs to friends, to the Levens's. They are coming here to start farming in a few weeks' time, and I am going into partnership with them. When my wife comes back from her holiday, we shall be moving up to Garthwen, the empty house you passed down the road.'

After a little persuasion, because he was a charitable and a lonely man, he gave in to our request for a night's lodging.

The kitchen was furnished in suburban style; there were horse brasses over the fireplace, a cheap dresser covered in orange and biscuit coloured pottery, and chintz-covered easy chairs. Gripping the frame of a Victorian picture of a snowy landscape was a small bird, a baby Little Owl. It clicked its beak at us in rage, opened its eyes until they seemed to be starting from its head, then swooped down on to one of the chairs where it lay on its back with curled talons in an act of juvenile aggression.

The man picked the bird up and nestled it against him, saying: 'I took him from the nest; he's great company and most affectionate. He's called Doom.'

2

There was a twilight gloom about the house that put me in mind of the sea-floor. The living-room faced east, and the westering sun shining full on the steep field rising from this back part of the house, threw a diffused light over walls and ceiling.

Hens and ducks scratched in the tiled hall, shaking out their feathers which sent up little clouds of fluff. Blinking their eyelids and moving their heads rapidly from side to side, they hovered in the doorway, hoping for crumbs.

A sun-radiant sheep lifted its head from grazing the mountain and wailed into the clear chasm between it and the house. Moved by its piercing cry, the three of us looked up from where we sat at table.

Stewart Hopkinson, the man of the house, invited us to remain a few days and to share his solitude.

'My wife is away,' he said briefly; walking about the room with the air of a lost being.

3

'Let us look at the abbey,' said Friedrich after tea.

It is a very meagre ruin, but the remaining walls are beautiful in age and atmosphere. The greyish green and bitter wormwood, a plant that grows by the gate at home and is picked by the mountain people as a remedy, here enriches the weathered stone. A narrow fissure cunningly built with a twist in the setting of the arch, squints in a slit-eyed vision of the sea.

A farmer and his son, both bearing heavy loads like sacks of sin, were passing in and out of the arched yard nearby. The wife was watching us intently, her head stuck out of an upstairs window, reminding me of when tramping through a crofting village in the Western Highlands, we saw the skylight of every cottage open and a head poke out to watch us. Up there, the women laughed and shouted to us in friendly greeting; the children sang out cheerfully. It was such a delicate humour, to stare like jack-in-the-boxes from their roofs instead of watching like common mortals from their doors. Here on the island the woman was silent as she peered from under the broken cardboard-mended panes. Cadwaladr's wife must have little cause for laughter in her life.

We looked in at the windows of the minister's recently vacated house. The furniture was still there, heavy brown leather chairs and sofa; there were books and papers spread over the table. We half expected to see the traces of a meal, so casually did the house seem to have been left. The minister having cleaned his neighbours' windows for the last time as a hint that they should not throw stones at glass houses, had walked out of his front door, padlocked the chapel, and with knobkerry in hand, had set sail for Africa and the saving of more tractable souls.

The island children had screamed their heads off for joy.

'By Christ and the Devil, the dog-collar has gone to the blacks!'

The men were delighted too; the minister had often accompanied them on the sea where because of his presence they were forced to curb their language. Above all, they were weighed down by the superstitious dread that his presence would bring disaster to the boat; for clergymen, corpses, and rabbits, bring bad luck to seamen.

From the north, one could see the whole island; a handful of farms, a lighthouse, a ruined monastery, an earth made fertile with the bones of men. The farm buildings, solidly made to withstand all weathers, had yards walled like fortresses. In the arch of a cart-shed at Pant was a stone bearing an incised sword or cross. The block had been built in lengthwise and had presumably come from the holy house.

The monastery stones had since the sixth century stood as a symbol of the human spirit, not only of religious faith but of escape as well. Men had fled here to live and to die, to begin a new life or to kiss the soil with the last touch of their withered mouths. It had always stood for freedom; now, in the modern sense, it stood for escapism too.

A rock shore; cliffs of mussel-blue shell. Wine-red, icy pink, pure white, yellow and green. The surf creamed at the foot of the coloured walls. Colours evoked images, images evoked words. Wall of jasper, tower of quartzite. How can a common seacliff be a wall of jasper? I would, knowing this salt channel and these bastions, make a new hymn to the virgin; say she was a wall of jasper with eyes clear as the running tide.

There was the solid wall, and round it ever-widening circles of association. For example, the south end of the island was linked with the memory of the Wild Cats. When the 'old people' moved off the island they left behind them all their cats. Having to fend for themselves, they became quite savage and grew to the size of small dogs from the success of their hunting. They would not go near the new inhabitants, except to raid their larders. They became such a menace to rabbit-trapping that they had to be exterminated, for unlike tame cats they did not kill one rabbit and eat it until they were satisfied, but went from body to body in the gins, eating only those succulent parts they particularly fancied.

At the bottom of Clogwyn land we discovered a blood-red cave, full of sea-anemones and egg-smooth pebbles, where years later I found the vari-coloured stone that became the 'wave-worn pebble burnt with sealight' dedicated to the feast day of Saint Rose of Lima.

In the late evening, as we sat on the grassy parapet that runs along the northern coast; among flowers, sea-pinks and vernal squills, we saw the young man we had watched earlier in the day near the monastery, disappearing round the mountain with a bucket for gulls' eggs.

At this northern end are black sea caverns. Above the caves the rock is white and worked over in raised veins, polished and fine as ivory. Some of these rock-veins were thin as spider web, others were thick as human arteries. The stone would seem to be composed of petrified tissues, skin, muscle, delicate bones. We ran our fingers over the filigree patterns. Falling to our knees, we touched the remains of our ancestors. Or their sculptured memorials in stone; their ivory-bright bird-bone perfection, the metamorphosed flesh. A valley of sun-whitened skeletons seen through a reducing mirror.

Why this preoccupation with stone, the framework of the earth? While turning over the soil here, a man might philosophise like the gravediggers in Hamlet. The second clown asks a riddle: 'Who builds stronger than a mason, a shipwright or a carpenter?'

And the first clown answers: 'A grave-maker; the houses that he makes last till doomsday.'

In every part of the island which is free of stone, the spade strikes against human thigh and breast-bone. In an island of only four hundred and forty-four acres, with half of that mountain and with reputedly twenty thousand saints buried there, it is understandable that certain areas of the earth should be thick with bones.

Under the eastern height men turn the remains of their ancestors when they dig; forking them over happily under the wide sky-benediction; for these are the bones of men who fulfilled themselves, who found realisation of visions in a fragment of land left miraculously to the air when other portions of this mountain range were submerged in the Pleistocene Age.

We turned southwards, walking to Ogof Lladron, where in a

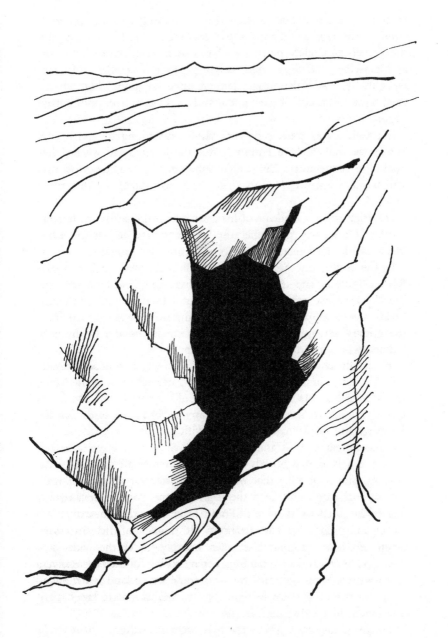

cirque of rock that on one side rises to a saddle, on the other to overhanging cliff, lies a snug and secret anchorage. I could imagine the French smugglers putting in here, swart men in stocking-caps and ear-rings, carrying their cargo of liquor up the precipice. Delightedly, the welcoming islanders used to guide them up to their farms, with talk of roast goose and duck; their eyes on the wine flagons.

A rough grassy track runs the whole way along the west side. While we walked there I mused over the lonely man we had left behind us in the house. He was like someone uprooted too violently, a man out of his place; highly strung and too unstable for this mode of life.

Friedrich began to tell me of his own loneliness, partly from over-burdened emotions, partly because for a few days he was to be out of the world, simplicity and peace loosening his tongue.

In the south, on the black rock of Pen Dinmor, Arthur of the Round Table is said to have been shipwrecked. The boat was lost but the king was saved. The legend has it that the king with torn breast, his royal garments salt-caked and stained, was dragged from the hungry sea by unknown hands and carried inland to the holy fathers, who tended his ragged wounds.

We caught sight for a moment of a tawny cat, one of those domestic animals left behind by families that had moved out. At this time, many homeless cats lived in the gullies of the south end. Island cats quickly revert to the wild, with many rabbits and birds for the hunting, and with much space in which to move freely, except for the danger of gins and snares.

This is a land that hoards its past and merges all of time in the present. The cargo boat that was salvaged last year off Maen Bugail, whose coal cargo will keep the island in fuel for the next twenty years; the illicit sweet wine of France; the shipwreck of Arthur; are of equal importance and freshness. It might be said that what happened here yesterday has taken on the colour of a long-past event, so timeless do happenings appear to be; as if the drama had been written long ago, and we who come by chance to the island play our parts that were designed for us, walking on to the stage at the twitch of a string held in the firm hand of the master.

Puppet strings took me by the hair-roots, drawing me back to the house in the quiet dusk; I had a sense of being forcibly drawn into the life of this elusive world.

It was almost dark by this time. A man in a peaked cap was sitting behind the door, his chair drawn back against the wall. The man had pale ginger hair and a white exhausted face.

'This is Merfyn, one of the lighthouse keepers,' said our host.

An hysterical, high-pitched laugh came from the mask behind the door. It was just possible to see his hands falling limply between his knees, from which hung a cloth bag holding full milk bottles.

After supper, when the two of us were alone, Hopkinson told me something of himself.

'I was brought up by foster-parents. Then I studied the law; while preparing for my examinations, I began to drink a lot of whisky and absinthe. I married Alice, and persuaded her to come here, over-looking that she has an Irish temper, and that she needs to go to a palais de dance every Saturday night. How she hates the sea! But real blind hatred. Now, she's gone off to the mainland to stay with her mother. I'm riding her on a loose rein in the hope that some day she will become resigned to this place.'

He paused to brood, with hunched shoulders.

'Last year, I threw up my law studies, and took this farm with the Levens's. We arrived in December, after a terrible crossing in which Alice lay flat on her back in the bottom of the boat. The house was no comfort; the bedrooms and living-room walls were running with moisture. The sheets and blankets felt like snails' beds. We were cut off from the mainland for four weeks after the day we arrived, and had to live on corned beef and potatoes. By the end of that time, Alice would not eat any more tinned meat. The islanders were not particularly friendly, either.'

4

Those first irradiant nights were like nothing I had ever experienced. Before getting into bed, I crouched at the window. There were no sash cords, so the frames were held open by pieces of stick. Across the slope of the mountain the lighthouse beam flashed like a scythe with stronger radiance than moonlight. Illuminating night: such innocence was in the cool winds and mooncast shadow. There was no nightmare, no dream. The house being in the middle of fields, took the full flash of the beams, the uninquisitive arcs passing over with a scythe's movements or like ground-lightning.

How different it was from those nights in Galloway, in the dark house above the Firth of Solway. That bedroom's leaf-heavy, tree-haunted gloom, where on entering, my heart felt the midnight shiver of massed foliage breathing and growing.

And the sea makes clean our hearts.

With the coming of full darkness, shearwaters began to shriek with the ghostly cries of dead men.

What had Stewart said during our long conversation? 'When I am out in the dark looking to my rabbit-snares, the shearwaters cry like banshees from their winding passages among the rocks.'

With the coming of first light, I would wash all over from a basin on the floor. Bending down in front of the small square of window I could feel the salt wind making me whole. The cows passed up the field into the main track on their way to be milked, with the timid hang-dog white bull limping slowly after them, hobbled and wretchedly impeded as he painfully dragged along his great bulk.

During the day, I walked from end to end of the island, Stewart's dog following me, moving foxlike through the high bracken of the eastern slopes. From the mountain-top the low land was small to the eye. In the simple unfoliated landscape where tawny stems break the horizontal lines of the low land, the fields were parcelled neatly into small squares of cultivation about an acre in extent; each field was surrounded by an earthen, grass-covered dyke, along the top of which it was pleasant to travel.

Every farm has its own withy bed for the making of lobster creels, but the beds have become so neglected in the past few years that withies have to be brought over from the mainland in the winter months.

Never had I seen ground so overrun by rabbits. They were a small variety, both grey and black and crosses of both, the black having been introduced by a lighthouse keeper. The fur of the black variety was long and of a silken fineness. Stewart, who had decided to experiment with the two breeds, had taken young rabbits out of his snares, tied string to the leg of each and pegged them down in the hope that they would breed.

5

I sat at Stewart's feet on top of a tall slab rearing from the sea. The cave, a narrow fissure always dark except at early morning when the sun shines in, was glutted through its narrow-necked entrance by the incoming tide.

Below us, a seal cow lay on her back in the bottle-green gloom of the cavern. With head out of water and flippers waving us to come down, down, to the depths of the sea, her brown eyes besought: Come to me, come to me. Her arms extended, folded again to her creamy underside. So great was the human mermaid attraction that I could have leapt to my death by drowning.

A woman on land and a silkie in the sea.

We had come with infinite caution down the precipitous holdless grass of the mountainside. Never before on any hill have I known such sheer grass. To slip a few inches, to lose the slightest control, would be enough to set a body rolling and bouncing over the cliffs into the waves. The wind was piercingly cold, so I had borrowed two of Stewart's sweaters and a pair of his old army trousers turned up in many folds, and a raincoat. By going barefoot, it was possible to move comfortably, digging heels and fingers into the turf. Below the awful expanse of grassy precipice came the ledges of firm and honest rock giving sound hold.

Our minds grew dazed by the thunder of the conflicting tides. As we let ourselves down the last yards where a few tussocks of thrift wait to crumble from the slope under unwary fingers, we came face to face with the Ancient Mariner. With bent knees and one hand against the rock he moved along a narrow lip made greasy with the droppings of birds. On his arm he carried a basket full of gulls' and razorbills' eggs bedded in fleece. Calmly plundering the hatcheries, with nothing but the assurance of balance to keep him from death, he moved warily and sinuously as a weasel. Swinging round with an extravagant gesture of alarm at sight of us above him, he nearly pitched forward over the rocks. He had been walking with his glass eye towards us. He was unshaven and his finger-nails were long, black, and hooked as talons.

Stewart called out harshly to him:

'This is a sanctuary for birds; you have no right to take so many eggs!'

For answer, he blew him a kiss, and touched an egg with his foot so that it rolled away over the edge of the precipice.

Deeply hurt, Stewart moved on, his cheeks and neck a deep red with mortification.

A hen and cock bird stood side by side, the mother bird sheltering her green egg between prehistoric feet. Having no nest in which to lay it, she guarded it against the soft wall of her belly. She cooed, nodded, danced, bowed, in reply to her mate. The cliffs murmured with their warm and mysterious communication. She was maternal and careless all at the same time. Feeling the need for a silver fish, she shuffled off the ledge, taking the egg with her.

'This stench is unbearable,' shouted Stewart. 'My God, how these birds do stink.'

Feeling like a pigmy, I climbed up and down among the crags. The sea was emerald, frothed with white. In lee of the land, submerged rocks of the reef showed as soft purple stains under the water.

We began to collect a few eggs while birds circled wildly round us. Herring gulls lay their eggs in shallow, primitive nests made of dead grass, feathers, sheeps' wool, or seaweed, along the rocky shore; or simply drop their eggs in depressions on the grass slopes. We found razorbills' eggs hidden in deep crannies. They were of a chalky white splashed with brown blotches the colour of old blood, and were more beautiful than the mottled dun-green eggs of the herring gull. Against the stones whitened with bird-droppings, they were perfectly camouflaged. Whenever we found a gull's nest with three eggs in it, Stewart broke one to test whether it was addled, for usually if the full clutch was there, it meant that the chicks had begun to form. When we had gathered about two dozen eggs for the making of omelettes, we hid them under a fleece ready to put into our bag on the way back to the west side.

After the chill currents of the sea-way, the breast of the island gave off an intense heat. Everywhere, birth was taking place; chicks were breaking from speckled shells under the burning-glass of the sun. On every shelving ledge, on hard-baked pockets of earth, whole eggs and green fragments of shell lay beside blind creatures beating the dust with embryonic wings. The gull king, his head hawklike between his shoulder blades, was watchful from eyes of cold amber. He alighted on the cliff, sea-water dripped from his beak of lemon bone. Around him squatted his clumsy off-spring.

The chipping of shells grew more insistent as the breeding sun gained its zenith. We trod with a sort of fear over the bald surface, stepping around new-born creatures and their shards.

There was an area rank with purple henbane, hollow-stalked flowers scarcely visible above shielding husks. The flowers, springing one above another on the stalk, were of a deadish yellow. The tough covering of the fruit of this soulless plant was like the husk of assarabacca, and in it was contained much small seed like poppy semen but with the colour of house-dust. Not only the root but the whole plant gave off a heavy smell that filled the surrounding air. This herb under Saturn draws melancholy humours from the region of the heart.

Sea parrots stood stiffly to attention at the mouths of abandoned rabbit-burrows, and as we approached, either drew back into the shelter of the holes or launched themselves with fiercely whirring wings down into the sea.

A pigeon with a shot-silk breast of bronze and green crouched on a limestone bluff and disregarded us. From the tilted stone platform, from the nesting ledges, there fell a constant shower of liquid excreta. The confused sound of love-making, scolding, and gossip, came from row upon row of bottle-shaped guillemots standing upright along the terraced walls. The cliff-face was spattered with the broken eggs that careless webbed feet had set rolling. Close to the water, shags were drying out their wings.

What fate overtakes each wave as it breaks against the land? I began to count, waiting for the seventh wave. How are we to know which is the first and which the seventh? How can we rationalise and set to numbers pulsations of water that have been world without end? A green wall of water advanced, only to spend itself and become diffused. Another and another followed it.

From clumps of bladder-campion we heard the cheeping of young birds and came upon a deep niche high in the cliff where chicks clamoured for food. I inserted myself in the entrance and wormed up into the darkness of the narrow cleft. When it became so constricting that I could push in no further, and when head was bent to the breast by the roof, I cautiously put out my arm into the dank air, to find that at full stretch I could feel inside the deep nest made of grass stems and wool; three, four, five pulsating heads. Their beaks gaped wide in a clamour for food. Carefully, I passed one chick down for Stewart to touch. It was a naked grey thing, with skeleton head and unfeathered wing-elements; pink-legged, pink-throated. After it had been returned to the nest, we retreated to the rocks below. Soon the parent birds returned; glossy, blue-black, bright-legged choughs. They fluttered with rustling wings on to the face of the cliff over the crevice, and after talking to their young and mobbing other birds that flew too near, flashed in to their chicks with loudly echoing cries.

In the height of the vault, black-backed gulls screamed at us, dropping close to our eyes with splayed talons. Wingless, grounded, our feet stumbled over pebbles, our faces burned in the oven-heat given off by dry rock. The air quivered, shaken as wind-disturbed water, making insubstantial the green headlands.

A bird power-dived. Alas, humankind; featherless, wingless, crawling the earth.

The whole east side resounded with the harsh anger of seafowl.

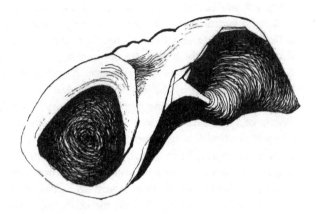

6

The waves were green, greenly came they, waves came ever-green out of Ireland, to fall upon the cliffs of Wales and glut her caverns with salt and broken things.

'There, quickly,' he said. 'Porpoise!'

A group of slug-backs rolled, curved up, disappeared, each behind the other as if there undulated a loch monster.

A little more faith O Lord, and I could walk on the water, or roll brightly gleaming like the basking shark.

'What really brought you here?' I asked Stewart.

'This seemed a wild place, and I needed wildness. The King is old and without a son so, who knows, I may be the next King or at the least, president of the island. Alice says she hates the life but summer is on the way, when things will be easier for her. She must learn to like it. Out in the world, what was I? But here, I stand a good chance of leadership.'

'Leadership: strange word.' A fanatic, an uncomfortable kind of man, burning himself out.

He was looking straight before him, his face severely secret. Did he ever, I wondered, peel away the protective covering when he was safe behind a locked door at the end of a corridor in the halls of loneliness? To a man perhaps; no woman would ever see his naked face.

After a little reflection he went on, 'Possibly I shall become a whole man in time, after my life and love have been simplified. If we lived in a tent, we could burn it down each spring and begin again.'

The sea was emerald, frothed with white. In lee of the island, the rocks of a submerged reef showed as purple stains under the water. Below us was the seal cave. Through a narrow fissure we saw the slimy ledges on which seals lie up, and the deep pool fed from the sea through a narrow-necked entrance. A seal cow was lying on her back in the gloom of the cavern. Her head was out of water. She waved her flippers, bidding us to come down to her. They were like fronds of weed floating loose from the heavy root of body. Something barked with a deep voice. It was the bull seal. Ah, there he went, smooth and black as oil, nine feet of solid flesh, twisting and rolling without a ripple to disturb the depths of the pool.

'He is almost twice as long as you are,' laughed Stewart.

Look, look, now he comes out, his black bull head dripping. One moment, he is in the stillness of the cavern; the next, he is in that boiling emerald sea. His nose is nobly acquiline, his heavy lids droop, hooding the eyes. He does not look directly at us, this bull seal, Leviathan. He will leave that to the cows of his harem. In the emerald, jewel-coloured sea, from the white foam-lace rise gentle stone-grey heads. Whiskered, human-eyed, they are the heads of his cows. They are dappled, white-breasted, their undersides seemingly vulnerable, gleaming as those of mackerel.

Ho there! beautiful beast. Moon-dappled silkie!

She twists to dive into the under-water tunnel leading to the pool, and where her back of mottled fur touches the surface, is iridescent as mother of pearl. Rainbow, mother of pearl, sheen of the sleek and mottled skin.

And the seal that wanted me to leap down into her arms—

'Look,' said Stewart. 'She is calling you again.'

'Come to me, come to me.'

From the deep pit, from the roof of whose galleries giant spiders hung spinning their white cocoons, in waning light, she sent messages of desire, that I should give myself to the sea and plumb the cold stillness of water under the rock. I leaned far over into darkening air; and her mild eyes spoke of human feelings. She took me down to my deepest roots nurtured on legend and fantasy. She told me that once I was a lonely woman living on a desert beach, without husband, without children; and if in the spring I was crowned it was with sea-tangle of my own wreathing. One day, she

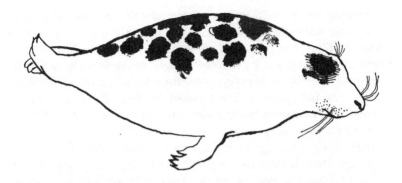

said, so great had been my desire to be a mother that I stole a baby
seal silken-haired and innocent, from a rock that spray blew over.
What a temper it had! It bit and scratched and tore its own face
furiously when it could not get at mine. It screamed with the voice
of any human child. The bereft cow roared and came up from the
surf to beat my door and windows with her flippers. She blew like a
whale through the keyhole; she moaned and whimpered for her
little bull. At last, she was forced by lack of success to go back to the
cold wastes of the sea; and I was left in peace. After a time, my
adopted child grew listless, the fight went out of it, and at last it
pined away, dwindling inside its long fur. It died; then, because
I feared the vengeance of its real mother, I went to live far away from
the seals' breeding ground.

O seal cow in the cavern; your mournful eyes.

Was it your baby I stole sometime in a former life? Rooted deeper
still in legend, I once married a stranger with whom I lived in great
contentment above the tidal ledge. I was happy enough until he
began to leave me for whole weeks with only turnstones and green-
shanks for company. But one night, when he had been away for a
long while, I went to the shore to gather driftwood by the moon's
light. A bull seal had risen from the sea and lay resting on a rock. He
was singing with a human voice, an old song, 'I am a man upon the
land, I am a silkie in the sea.'

The shock of it made me scream; and hearing me, he gave a great
bellow of disgust because I had seen him as he really was, and
flapped away into his true element away from me for ever.

In truth, and quite apart from the weaving of legends, a bull seal sometimes shows sexual interest in women when they are swimming near him; particularly in fearless young virgins. For instance, I have when bathing at night in the company of young people among a herd of seals, and a girl has stood upright in the water, seen a bull seal swim rapidly to her with powerful interest, stare into her face and at the last moment dive between her legs. There is often so strong a link between woman and seal that it would seem almost normal for them to co-habit.

Stewart left me, to go back along the shore in search of Friedrich, who had been daunted by the steepness of the grassy precipice, and whom we had not seen for the past hour. He was a long time gone.

Evening has come: it is cold on this sunless rock. Waves toss tumultuously past the shore. The pool grows more and more mysterious, and a stench rises from the sleeping-ledges. The old black bull seal snorts at me from somewhere below. A pale moon rises in the wind-burnished sky. I sit and sit alone with the waves, the creatures and the stones.

The sea pours relentlessly past, the sea is cold: the white moon is cold also, a virginal spring moon. I do not move at all on top of my rock so that birds fly close and show their bellies, trailing feet, and clear eyes. But I do not see the razorbills' eyes; they are too small and black. They would seem to be blind, so small and black are their eyes against the dark plumage.

The bull seal snorts below in the darkness; it is a cold desolate sound, filled with repugnance. He wishes I would go away.

Stewart does not come, and I am surrounded on one side by water, on the other by blocks of stone.

To the left, there is the rock wall a few inches from my head; to the right, I can see a few yards as far as the corner round which birds circle. If Stewart does not come back I shall wait until the moon has gained mastery in the sky, and then climb the cliff and find my own way home to the stone house in the middle of the island.

I am cold; I am happy. Not until the moon is high—there, the signal from the gulls! He is returning, for the birds have risen and gone seaward over the waves. Head and shoulders first, then the whole figure moves among the rocks. He raises an arm in greeting and I smile, being comforted on my cold throne. I smile, going back in memory to an evening in childhood when walking near

Gorad, a boat passed in slack water and those aboard her raised hands in benediction.

Salutation to the shores of worlds.

On a shelf above the cave were tunnels dug in curiously powdered grey soil that contained much bird excreta. Stewart opened one of the tunnels with his knife, hoping to find a shearwater in it, but it was empty. One hole went down into the soft crumbly earth. I dropped a stone into it, and heard the faint splash about thirty feet below in the cave pool. We had to tread carefully, as there was a danger of the earth giving way beneath us at any moment.

From the summit ridge we looked westward to where the sunset was falling into grey ash. The lamp suddenly burned in the eye of the lighthouse, its beam beginning to play over the twilit fields.

We could see Friedrich's figure far below, standing at the side gate of Pen Craig, waiting for us. He had been overcome by vertigo on the steepest part of the east side and had with great difficulty on hands and knees dragged himself back up the slope, with a swimming head. He was silent and shaken, and said very little when we rejoined him.

After supper, yawning, stretching, on the hard wooden chair, with night flowing past the window, I had to listen to a continuation of the story of Stewart's life. Friedrich had gone to bed, saying he was a bachelor and unused to late hours.

'It was grim,' said Stewart, 'to live in the shadow of two guardian aunts.' He mused for awhile, then spoke again.

'The great thing in life is desire, or as some prefer to call it, Love,' he pronounced.

'Love, desire, poetry. Women and poetry.' He plucked an imaginary guitar.

Women with thighs the colour of meadowsweet; and maidenhair crisp as fern. Darkness of the navel in the smooth belly. Where the string has been, it is dark, it is empty. All of us, with severed, perished navel strings, desire the mother from whom we were cut by the scissors of a nurse. We desire the breast and the womb even after our beards are grown. In the beginning it is: Mother, carry me; I am tired. In the long middle period: Hold me in your arms, beloved. At the last: Raise me a little on the pillow to see the sun.

Women wash mother's blood from us when we are born, and wash the world's dirt from us after we are dead.

39

I listened carefully, as if it was important that I should be his confessor; and watched the man's thin, sickly, and unhappy face. There was an awkwardness in his gestures but when speaking in the heat of memory, he lost self-consciousness.

7

Overnight, the force of the wind made the base of Craig y Llanw and Maen Bugail hoary with foam. Wind raved through the house, chilling us. We were partially sheltered by the mountain, but on the other side of the island, one of those waves running through the Sound at the flood would have swamped the small island boats.

After a breakfast of seagulls' and ducks' eggs, we went to the anchorage to see if there was any possibility of getting across to the mainland. Cadwaladr was out lifting his lobster pots at the south end.

On the wall of the boat-house dogfish hung drying for bait. Under a derelict boat, the vertebrae of a whale bleached and growth-ringed lay in company of a rotting hide of a red cow. Each man had his own private corner in the boat-house, where he kept his outboard engines, oilskins, lobster-creels, and ropes. Rolled sails were stowed away under the beams. An ancient tattered sail, massive oars, and a mast bigger than any of the others, belonged to the old black boat, the communal craft that had belonged to the old islanders, the men of memories, men of faded photographs; bearded, in tam o' shanters, taller than men are now; more heroic, removed from the present into saga-land by the passage of time.

The lobster fishers came in with their catch, and told us that judging from the state of the seas round the island it would be impossible to cross the Sound for a day or so.

O joy, another day with the seals.

I thought, how cosy it must be in winter, securely cut off from the world outside.

By evening, the gale was deadly in its shrivelling coldness; but Friedrich who had lain all day in a sheltered coign of rock in Porth Clegyr, was burnt by the sun. He had lain on the white beach of wave-pounded shell like Jonah, spewed up out of the whale's dark stomach.

8

As we prepared supper, I called out to Stewart,

'I have a friend, a Frenchman, who would like this sort of life.'

Friedrich came to the kitchen door, stiff with disbelief and disapproval.

'Paul?' he asked. 'Surely, he would find it too quiet?'

'No,' I said. 'No, I am going to tell him about it.' I pretended more conviction than I felt.

I fed Stewart's pet lamb, and shivered in the piercing blast that poured out of the east.

Friedrich said: 'This wind comes from Asia, from the steppes.'

At home in the mountains, the leaves of the elder bushes would be hanging withered too soon after their unfolding. On the island, there was scarcely a tree to suffer; but the potatoes had been unearthed and thrown about the ground by the force of the wind, despite the fact that the gardens were protected by high walls.

After midnight, in what remained of the hours of darkness, I dreamt. There was a dense sea-fog; and there was a woman staring into a dark mirror, for judgement. Her expression was evil. She was whispering to herself with a sound like tearing cloth. She appeared to be my stepmother, and was perfecting herself in the learning of Black Arts. In the elastic space and time of the dream, years passed like the turned pages of a book. For a year and a day she saw nothing more mysterious than the dim shadows of her room, the rapier glances of her own eyes; the milk and carmine of her own flesh. Another year went by. She was incapable of any but evil thoughts. A web of smoke began to form in the glass. At the end of two more years, fog was swilling about the room. The woman's patience was her deadliest weapon. Towards the end of the seventh year a head had materialised in the fog. On the seventh day after the seventh year her spell was perfected. She called for me and the other children to appear before her. How reluctant we were to breathe the stale air of her apartment.

'I have no use for you,' she said. 'You shall be neither fish nor beast from now on. Get along with you to the sea; but first, take a look at yourselves in my mirror.'

We peered into the glass; round, whiskered heads, fat ungainly bodies, helpless flippers. We fought and writhed to get away from the sight of one another.

The dream changed; I was still a seal, but I came to the surface of a glittering night-sea and felt the moon's calm eye shining on mine, drawing me up. I took a deep draught of air knowing I might spend a night and a day in human shape. Throwing off my skin, I became a woman. Chance had brought me to an islet, which at first seemed to be uninhabited. No, a man was wandering there alone over broken blocks of stone. He stopped when he saw me sitting there. He was afraid to approach me; so at dawn I went to him saying, all night I was watching you.

He told me of his fears, of his loneliness. We walked hand in hand over the ribs of rock, over petrified bone and sun-dried tissue of bird. He begged and begged to know the truth about me. I told him my father ruled the floor of the ocean, that my mother had liked to gather shells to bring back to me where I swung in my weed-roped cradle. One day she had been overtaken by a sea-eruption, and buried alive in lava-dust. My father was mad with despair, wandering the sea-bed until he came to the cave of a wise-woman, who flattered him and comforted his body so that he lost the power of reasoning. This woman had changed me into a white-furred seal and had driven me out to the sea.

It was the end of my time on earth; I began to run towards the water, pulled by a magnet stronger than any human could use to ensnare me. The man followed me down, swimming powerfully, but his strength gave out; and as I went in at my father's door the young man, already one of the green dead, floated by the open window.

Waking to sunshine, to the light-sounds of bird and sheep, I was absolved from black fantasy; and from the evidence of torn paper and tiny droppings of dirt on the floor, knew that mice had inspired my dreams.

The islandmen were gathered in the anchorage, preparing to cross to the mainland with crabs, lobsters, and gulls' eggs. A black stove was carried down and dumped in iron desolation on the beach, ready to be put into the dinghy. Shellfish is taken to the village three times a week. To keep the catch alive and fresh until it is transported, the fishermen store the shellfish in wooden 'keeps' in which air holes have been drilled. These boxes are lodged in the rocks and covered with seaweed; they are kept in places where the tide will cover them once a day.

To this simple shore on which the stove speaks of domesticity (the sea however loved cannot stand for home) I feel my roots begin to cling. On this shore, among these peasants, a man and woman could give all they had to the combined work of their hearts. There must be a house to live in, a fire for the entertainment of friends, an open door for the chance seafarer. On one hand, there must be the spaces of purple and olive water; on the other, straight-rising chimney-smoke of a quiet house. At the core, must be the justification of life, the work for which they are fitted.

A miserable icy rain numbed us as we waited for the many boxes of writhing crabs to be stowed in sacks. Twm's father-in-law, an old man suffering from a weak heart, waded out to the dinghy in cracked boots that let in the water. He and his friend, another old man from the mainland, lifted in the iron stove, and the Ancient Mariner threw aboard a bundle of dirty clothing. Next, he handed in a weight from a weighing machine. A brooding expression came on the father-in-law's face as his arm took the pull of the iron. Growing more and more thoughtful, he slowly lowered it to the bottom of the boat.

With the dinghy in tow and two men in her, we slipped out of the Cafn. The foxy bitch ran, a-shiver and whimpering for as long as she could keep abreast of us. As we coasted towards the Sound, she raced up and down the headland, barking after her master. With cynical aloofness the Ancient Mariner watched us go.

The rain was chilling. In long grey shrouds the resting-place of the holy fathers fell away. Already it was the past: time had not after all stood still. The seal cave dropped astern; the yellow-stained rocks, the ledges lined with sober birds, vanished. The sheltering cliffs slid backwards. The tide rip of the Sound was under us and around us. How deep and savage was the sea, how cramped our craft. We were sprayed with salt and switchbacked over those waves that spouted so viciously. The dinghy tossed in our wake.

For as long as they could see it, my eyes did not leave the rain-shrouded mountain. On her slopes I had left a new self, and had vowed to return.

Off the opposite shore towards Braich y Pwll, porpoise were rolling, a sign of more settled weather.

We did not make directly for the village beach, but first put in at a sheltered cove, Porth Ancr, so that the old men could take off their stove.

We slipped into summer; the water inshore was calm and trans-lucent. Light broke in a great splendour of colour over the inland heights.

Friedrich was disillusioned. He had expected some fairy quality in the island, a dreamlike perfection, a mode of existence lifted above life. He had wanted to sink himself in the past; to walk a Celtic shore, led on by long-footed maidens with anaemic faces; to be handed in and out of boats by bowing-from-waist boatmen versed in the utterances of Taliessin: in short, to be treated as Herr Professor and as Toff. He may even for all I know have considered the bestowal of strings of beads upon the natives. The rude and grasping present he found distasteful.

The final ugliness came when Twm smiling with suave greed named as the price of our crossing there and back the sum of three pounds.

TWO

THE RETURN

I

CAN I dare plunge into the hermit-life, into the fisherman farmer's narrow existence?

I, I, I, ram-horned battering at the holy isle, at the mocking-rock of the seal cave in the east; at the sly bays of the south west; at the Merlin-haunted child-sized fields.

What am I? Whence did I come? Whither shall I go? Among rock-bones in the deeps of the muscular ocean?

Old sea, make our hearts fresh!

Take no heed of the world's weather; remember well, that storm batters at each man's heart.

Waking to sunshine, to the light-sounds of bird and sheep, I am absolved from dreams of a treasure island, and the Loadstone of Balnibarbi.

2

Hot eventless hours dragged by under the sun which had burnt away all colour from the sea. Two island boats were anchored in the bay and a green-painted dinghy lay sideways on the sand. Under the wall built to prevent the churchyard from disintegrating into the waves, the islanders had stacked boxes of shellfish and were selling them to the poulterer who came once a week from the nearest market town to buy their catch. Metal-blue lobsters lay under seaweed to protect them from the sun's white rays. Pink-brown crabs, some small as a hand, others massive-clawed and calloused, peered at the glittering drought of the world from pinpoint eyes.

I had arrived about noon in the village and had carried my gear into the post office. I enquired whether Mr. Hopkinson's boat was expected over from the island. The postmaster stared past me at the wall, then with a swift turn of the head, glanced up at the face of the clock behind him and said:

'Yes, they should be over any time now. It is the day for lobsters.'

So I had walked to the furthest point of the bay, to see the ghost-shape of the island miles away to the sou' west like a giant rat with arched back and extended tail.

In the early afternoon, a black spot had appeared off the opposite headland, stayed in sight for a few seconds, and vanished again.

'A hundred, a hundred and one, a hundred and two, and three for luck . . .'

A small shadow moved under the cliffs; then it became two boats and a dinghy in tow. As they ran towards the shore, making their way carefully round submerged rocks, I saw Hopkinson, and waved to him.

The men transferred themselves from the anchored motorboat into the dinghy and sculled swiftly ashore. Hopkinson was the first to leap out into the surf. With loud guttural cries the others followed him as a comber lifted the stern of the light craft and threw it clumsily towards the beach. As it skimmed the top of a wave the men on either side plunged forward, their hands clasped to the gunwales. They grounded the boat safely on the sand; then with cries of 'Heave' began to carry it above high water mark. Hopkinson, like a man on stilts, his long thin legs emphasised by waders, came up to me.

'How are you?' I asked, happy with relief that the boat had come.

'Bearing up,' he answered, with an embarrassed grin adding, 'My wife's back; and our furniture arrived last week, but the house is still untidy.'

The glare from sea and sky was blinding on the whitewashed walls of the houses. The islandmen were tramping back and forth with meal-sacks, coal, and provision boxes. I sat on the coping of the bridge over a small stream mouthing its way into the sea through the middle of the village. Hopkinson smiling wearily, weighed down under a sack of coal, passed but said nothing.

Towards evening the wind freshened, the sky becoming streaked with wisps of white storm cloud. The men seemed never to have done with carrying sacks and tins of petrol. At last, around seven o'clock, a stranger came up to me and said, 'They're going now. Where is your gear?'

Hopkinson was standing at the water's edge. Wordlessly, he picked me up and carried me out to the dinghy. With the other men, he threw himself aboard and crouched in the stern to scull the craft out with violent movements of the shoulders.

The other boat was already far ahead, its white sail like a bird flying towards its home beyond the Sound. We transferred ourselves to the motor boat; as I climbed over the gunwale, Hopkinson said to me,

'I'll be behind in the dinghy. I'm going to fish on the way back.'

The dinghy was secured behind, a scarlet sail was hoisted, and the spar braced from the stern-sheets by a boathook. The engine was started and for the second time, my land life was snapped. The white bird far ahead to the southward tacked into shadow. Our scarlet sail took the last of the sun on her wings. One man, seated under the fat belly of the sail, had a fringe of whiskers on his pirate cheekbone.

Hopkinson held a mackerel line out over the stern of the dinghy. He leaned away, then suddenly whipped round in triumph, a silver fish writhing in his fist. Laughing, he waved it above his head, the fish's blackish blood running between his fingers, before throwing it into the scuppers. After rebaiting his hook, he looked up at the burning red of the canvas and smiling, turned away.

It took us an hour and a half to make the six mile crossing. By the time we slipped into the anchorage out of the strong drag of the flood tide, the white wing of the other boat had already been folded and the crew had disappeared to their homes.

I was aware once again of the unearthly peace of the island, wearing a deceptive summer evening innocence. The hay fields were tall with sunburnt grass and flowers. There was neither sight nor sound of humanity in the clover-sweet air. It was a quiet green world of rough pasture, bracken and gorse; but underneath were the sea-caverns into which, at times of storm the surf would burst like gunfire. It was familiar, this world that had so far been just outside the range of my actual experience. Many sea-ancestors moved strongly in me.

Stewart spilled words as we walked together up the track.

'Alice said she would leave me again for good if you set foot here again,' he said. 'She can't bear the place and she's jealous of you because you seem to like it.'

We passed the garden wall of his house; glancing up at the windows, we both fell silent.

At the end of the lane stood a grey house facing the south.

'Do you think you'll be all right, yonder?' he asked.

We pushed our way past a tangle of weeds and dense fuschia bushes towards the door, where the threshold was covered in fallen petals. The front door hung on one rusty hinge leaning into an empty room.

'It's very rough,' he said. 'I'll bring you a pan and brush to sweep the dirt from the floors.'

We entered the quiet dust-filled house, in all of whose rooms were imprisoned birds, butterflies, and big downy moths beating their cobweb-covered wings against the closed windows or fluttering helplessly about the floors. I left the outer door ajar and opened the windows: the freed creatures fluttered out into the air and were carried away on the fresh aerial currents.

I wandered from room to room upstairs. It began to grow dark. The bedroom was foul with decay; there was a hole in the ceiling; dry-rot in the floor under the window; a smell of cobwebs and decay. Through the blurred window I could see the path and the roofs of Garthwen House and its out-buildings.

Hopkinson had sent me letters full of his plans for the future, and of encouragement of my own idea for settling on the island. Now Alice was back, he was a stranger.

The lamp was lit in the lighthouse as the sun went down into the western sea. I spread my sleeping bag on the floor and formed my spare clothing into a pillow. Strips of mouldy paper lay about; the walls were pocked with a damp rash. A fine wind began to moan through the house.

At first, I could not believe in the sound that grew with the wind. The house was inhabited by choristers! The young voices rose and fell in plain-chant. It was possible clearly to differentiate between the voices. The spot where they were singing was situated between the front room and the kitchen, near the doorway. There was comfort in having such friendly ghosts in the house. It grew dark; and still Hopkinson did not come back as he had promised.

Since earliest childhood, I was never able to sleep at night without first making my peace with God. For this, it was necessary to forgive and be forgiven; so I put on my jacket, and went to Garthwen; not by the pathway but through the fields, being afraid of meeting anyone on the way. I climbed an iron gate out of a weedy meadow and approached the back door of the house. A light was shining in the kitchen window. I knocked, and heard an exclamation inside.

Hopkinson called out, 'Come in.'

He and his wife were seated before the empty grate in a small room.

'Mrs. Hopkinson, I had to come and see you.'

Stewart's wife was older than I had expected her to be; she had an attractive face, but her body was slack and heavy. She flung down the newspaper she had been reading, and pushing back her chair, thrust her face close to that of Hopkinson.

'I don't know what sort of stories my husband has been telling you about me.' She suddenly shouted at the man who sat completely still.

'Well, Hopkinson, what have you got to say for yourself? Are you dumb, or deaf?'

Turning to me, she said, 'I'm not angry with you. It's this lying coward here. Oh, I'm through with him, I'm through.'

The man said quietly, 'You had better go. It won't do any good to stay.'

'Very well. Good night.'

He followed me. 'I told you how it would be,' he said without reproach. 'Sometimes, I think she must be mad.'

'It's easy to think that, when you don't understand someone.'

'She must be mad or ill,' he protested. 'She has not been well, lately. Neither of us can sleep. What a state to be in.'

'What will she do now?'

'Heaven knows, but she threatened to sleep at the other farm if you came back. She will have the island humming with scandal by morning.'

'I've dreamed for weeks of this day; of being free of everyone I knew before . . . to be able to sit quite alone and think without interruption.'

The back door opened. Alice came out towards the gate into the courtyard. She was wearing a pale blue overall. Staring straight ahead, she went away into the courtyard. The man groaned, 'Oh my God, she's gone to tell the neighbours.'

'Does she think I'm running after you?'

'Something of the sort, I suppose,' he said slowly.

'I had hoped you were going to make something fine out of living in this place.'

'So did I,' he said with a grimace. 'But I'm beginning to doubt. You have your work. That's something. As for me, if this fails, everything goes.'

There was a footfall in the stackyard, a whiteness near the gate. Alice was coming back. Wordlessly, she walked between the two of us, shut the garden gate after her and entered the house. The key was turned in the lock.

'What will you do if you can't get in?'

'I'll be able to get in; don't you worry,' he reassured me. 'You had better try to get some sleep,' he urged. 'The longer we stand talking out here, the worse it will look to Alice.'

So I went back to the dark house, but found it impossible to sleep. It was long past midnight.

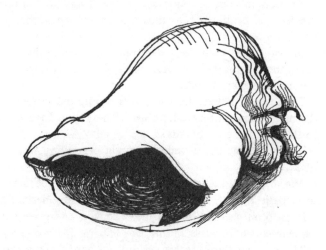

3

There was a loud knocking at the front door, the blows ringing hollow through the unfurnished rooms. I found my voice and called out.

'It's me, Hopkinson,' he answered.

'What do you want?'

'May I come up? Have you got a light?'

'No, but there's a candle somewhere.'

I felt about the floor for matches, helped by the flashes of the lighthouse beam that scythed across the floor from the uncurtained windows.

'Whatever do you want at this time of night?' I burst out, when the man appeared. 'It must be after one o'clock. When I heard you knocking at the door, I was sure the islandmen had come to drown me.'

'They would not do that,' he protested. There was no chair in the room, so he stood awkwardly near the fireplace. Dirt-covered cobwebs clung to his face and tore away in his hair.

'Christ,' he exclaimed, reacting as if the webs had been hands clutching at him. 'What a place.'

'Why aren't you in bed? It's so late.'

'Alice sent me to bring you to sleep at Garthwen.'

'What! Alice sent you?'

'We couldn't rest . . . Anyway, you can't stay here in this dirt. Get dressed and come to the house. She's getting a room ready for you.'

Uneasily, the man looked round the candle-shadowed room. 'Ugh, these cobwebs.' He beat upwards, and his fingers came away meshed in sticky strands.

'I can't bear spiders,' he said. 'Alice would die if she had to spend the night alone in a derelict house. Surely, you have not been able to sleep on the bare boards?'

'You woke me up,' I lied. 'I thought everything was over for to-night.'

'We've just had a fearful row. Have you seen the moon? It's the most perfect night, so peaceful . . . Isn't life wonderful?'

Hopkinson peered down at me. 'Did you eat? Have you had any supper?'

'No, nothing since breakfast. I did not have the appetite.'

He eyed with disfavour the damp-mottled red walls, the crack in the plaster over the fireplace.

'Alice is making up a bed for you.' He crossed the floor to the window; pushed back the sliding centre frame, and sniffed the night.

'So peaceful, it's unbelievable,' he sighed. 'Are you coming?'

'No.'

'Please; she's ashamed of herself at last. You won't believe it, but

Alice has a tender heart. She was upset at the thought of your sleeping up here. She would never dare to sleep alone in a house.'

'I'm used to living alone.'

'I told her you were scared.'

'That's not true.'

'Never mind. Tell her you were too scared to sleep alone, and she'll come round. You'll see.'

He paused to light a cigarette. 'Come along,' he coaxed. 'I'll go downstairs while you are dressing.'

He was waiting for me in the dining-room. Moonlight latticed the floor. Through the wide window the rapid flashes of the lighthouse beam picked out an eye, a piece of crumbling plaster, a door handle. Fuschia bushes, tangled across the path leading to the porch, seemed to have come closer in the darkness. Their blossoms heavy with nectar peered into the room.

'Let's be going if you are ready,' he said, walking to the door and brushing aside the flowering boughs so that I could follow him. Outside, was sanity and coolness after the stale air of the upstairs room. Across the mountain the beam of the distant lamp was brighter than the moonlight. Illumination, calm and impartial. There was a scarcely-felt sea-wind. The muffled swell beat time with the pulse of my own heart. Shearwaters cackled; a thousand blasphemous cries, weaving invisible flights between the stars and the earth.

At Garthwen the light still burned in the kitchen window; there was also a candle shining upstairs. Hopkinson opened the back door and stood aside for me to pass. With head cocked to one side, he called nervously.

'Alice?'

'Yes,' a stifled, equally-nervous voice answered from upstairs.

'Go and sit down,' he said, pushing me towards a wicker armchair in which a tortoiseshell kitten lay asleep.

'Sit down,' he repeated. 'Here, Puss, out you go.' He smiled, as if to reassure himself, and left me. I picked up the kitten and began to stroke its soft thin body. They were murmuring together upstairs. From the flat sound of Alice's voice I could guess that her anger was spent and had been succeeded by exhaustion. Hopkinson came downstairs again, and began to lay the table.

'Alice will be down in a minute,' he said. 'She is making up a bed for you.'

From somewhere in the house a clock chimed two.

'Good lord, no wonder I feel tired,' yawned the man. 'Do you like sardines?' he asked, opening a tin and putting it on a plate in the middle of the cloth.

As he cut bread and butter, he spoke lightly of the weather and the prospects for hay harvest.

He called out, 'Supper's ready.'

As if she had been waiting for the signal, Alice immediately entered the room. Her face was fully visible to me for the first time. She looked desperately tired, ill, and unhappy, with black smudges under the eyes. Her short dark hair was unkempt and dull. Seating herself at the table, she stared indifferently into space. The lower lids of Hopkinson's eyes were heavy-pouched, but the pupils had not lost their habitual, almost feverish brightness. He watched his wife, a look of desperate anxiety on his face. At intervals he said, 'You aren't eating anything,' a collective remark to both of us. A small phial of tablets lay beside Alice's plate; a similar one stood at the man's right hand.

'Have you taken your pill?' he asked his wife. She shook her head.

'Come on,' he urged. 'You need it. See, I'm taking mine.' He put a tablet in his mouth and washed it down with a sip of tea.

Listlessly, Alice copied him.

'If you've had enough to eat, I'll show you to your bedroom,' said Hopkinson.

Sleep would not come. In their bedroom across the passage, the husband and wife kept up a monotonous conversation until the sky greyed into morning.

At breakfast time, Hopkinson tapped at the door.

'Here's a cup of tea and a basin of water,' he called out.

Alice was getting up from the table when I got down. She said good morning almost gaily. From the yard came the sound of an axe on wood.

'My husband is chopping firewood,' laughed Alice. 'He always does that to relieve his feelings. He's quite crazy, you know. Last night, when I went out to shut up the fowl house, he thought I was going to sleep at the next farm.'

Presently Hopkinson came in; said an abrupt good morning to me, and sat at table. Leaning over him to pour tea into his cup, Alice put her left hand on his shoulder; pressing her fingertips into his shirt so fiercely that he winced from the pain of the nails in his flesh. He glanced up furtively at his wife, who smiled blandly on him.

'You've got your job for this morning, haven't you?' she asked.

Only when he reluctantly replied, 'Yes,' did she release his shoulder.

4

I escaped from Garthwen to the west side. It was a calm morning with a flat ocean; a morning of blue and gold, with heavy frost-like dew. I hid among the rocks like a beast, to lick my wounds. I peered into dense weed-forests gripping precipitous slopes rising from the sea-bed. I touched the crust, the stone-hard patina of silver and platinum rock-pools in which lay hard blue mussels and rooted soft anemones; mounds of red flesh from whose wine-deep hearts ever-moving tentacles stretched towards the sun. Acorn barnacles and limpets shone through the clear green water. On the rocks at the tide-edge oyster-catchers screamed from orange bills, lifted bright legs at my approach, and circled with flashing black and white wings. A breeze darkened the wave's breast, the peacock fan.

At the entrance to a deep cave, a bull seal fished, his body green as glass when he dived underwater. Beyond him, the tide-rip was smooth as black marble.

I would live alone in one of the abandoned houses, Ty Bychan, cutting myself completely free of Hopkinson and his wife. After a few days the loss of Hopkinson's friendship would become dulled by my absorption in work.

When I got back to the empty sunlit farm, I noticed how the breeze had refreshed the rooms. A small bird had come in since last night and was fluttering about the floor. I shared its joy when at last it flew away.

5

Terror. Violence. Greed. I was not passing over to a dream life, an escapist's paradise, but to one that whitened the hair and bowed the back, that would raise sea-monsters of hatred and despair.

It was all so familiar, this world that was just outside life; my ancestors never having worked so strongly as they did now in me. I found that I was beginning to belong to the sea. It was familiar and yet stranger than dream.

The island wore a deceptive summer innocence like a flower garden in which a serpent lay asleep. The fields seemed innocent; the mountain-back was never anything but its indifferent rocky self, dry and forbidding, with boulders lonely and savage, stinking from guano. There was scarcely ever the sound of a human voice on the clover-sweet air. There was nobody about. It was as well not to be deceived; the serpent was awake and watchful from frosty eyes. Only cows and sheep; but the single cart track ran the gauntlet of all the farms, and houses have windows and windows have eyes.

A man came by to look over the sea into the west. He saw wood smoke rising from my kitchen chimney. Dai Penmon, who had been in to light my fire and to sweep rubbish from the floors, went on his bandy-legged way home. He stopped to speak with the man. I saw this other middle-aged heavy man, powerful in the twilight, leap forward with astonishment to peer up at the face of the house. I heard his curses, his exclamations of astonishment. Long afterwards his wife told me how he had come back to their farm up the lane and had said to her, 'That woman's here again, all by herself in the next house.'

'And I couldn't rest in my bed for worrying about you,' she said.

6

Between my temporary home and the next farm, Pant, where Tomos
Bull-neck lived with his black-browed wife, ran what became for me
the Sacred Way; a wide grassy lane between stone walls. The lane
widened into a weedy court overpowered by the ruin and the tall
crosses and slate-topped sarcophagi on which was draped every
Monday morning the Pant washing. Impaled on the brambles that
hid the further tombs were discoloured rags of underwear. Calves
grazed among the tombs.

In the yard was an old boat and in her fitting up an old engine was
Cadwaladr Tomos with a cap pulled over his eyes. When I knocked
at the back door, iron-rimmed clogs sounded inside. The woman
who had watched us from her bedroom window when I was here
with Friedrich came to the door. It was Nans, wife to the boat-
building Cadwaladr. Her daughter Siani watched us round the crack
of an inner door. Cadwaladr followed us in, tossing his cap on to a
sea-chest near the fire. His presence was oppressive; the woman and
child watched him apprehensively as if he had been a stoat and they
rabbits. The weight of his presence fell like a blight or a bewitch-
ment on the household.

7

By bush telegraph it went round that Stewart's wife was threatening
to leave him again. The man chopped wood from dawn to dark in
the gloomy farmyard beside the house, as a relief to his feelings.

On the first Wednesday in the month, the lighthouse ship which
calls here once a month with a change of keepers and to bring
provisions, coal and oil to the lighthouse brought also the Levens
family, furniture and food.

Alice met them on the beach; she flung herself sobbing into the
arms of Zöe Levens, and poured out the story of what she felt of
hatred for the island while the ship's crew listened with interest.

The man Levens was mild and unambitious. He had given up his
work as an engineer in order to fulfil his dream of becoming an
islander. He had no previous experience of farming, but he intended

to raise cattle and sheep and pigs. He knew every stone of the place which he had grown to love over many years of summer holidays.

His wife was small and lively and self-assertive, inimical to the island but, since she could not move her husband from his desire to be a farmer, determined to make a success of her new life.

They had two sons, Harold and Douglas, and a baby daugher Vera. It was in their house that Friedrich and I had stayed with Stewart when we first arrived. Levens and Hopkinson had planned to farm together the lands of Garthwen and Pen Craig, but Alice was so unsuited to the life that the plan had had to be abandoned.

8

At this point, in ignorance and under the careful and constant flattery of the Bull-necks, I was made to break the balance of power then ruling island politics. Almost without realising it, I found that I had taken sides for the Bull-necks and their one or two friends such as Dai Penmon, the young lobsterman, and against the Rest who were only names to me in those first few days. By careful insinuation Cadwaladr led me to believe that the rest of the community was un-favourable to my presence, and that there was no merit in getting to know the King, the Jacob Lloyds, the Twm Clogwyns, or the family Ancient Mariners. Alice and Stewart Hopkinson being comparative new-comers, were not proscribed by him. It was part of his master-plan to have a close alliance with at least one family from whom he could obtain inside information of the enemy camp. At the moment, the Hopkinsons supplied this link.

So I became a rebel without knowing what the war was about; and became a cause of great annoyance to the people on 'the other side'.

Cadwaladr played on my weakness and sense of insecurity, on my ignorance of the true state of affairs between him and his neighbours, and on the embarrassment now existing between me and Hopkin-son. By suggestive prompting he made it impossible for me to make overtures to the other men and women, they were the unknown persecuting the good old man, the venerable long-suffering Cadwal-adr. He made it appear that they were ready to persecute me too, totally without reason except that they resented strangers in their midst. He made it plain: only the enlightened Bull-necks embraced change and new faces; only the Bull-necks were human. How innocent I was in those days! Cadwaladr had the fish securely by the gills, and the little fish felt nothing but a vague unease, and continued to nibble contentedly at the bait.

9

The family at Pant having begun to show an excessive friendship for me, I was unable to lock or even to shut my front door against them; and it became customary to find two or three of the family in or about the house when I came back from painting. Sometimes the younger son Tudur would be waiting on his heels against the wall in one of the empty rooms, with a gift of a live crab; or his mother would be waiting in the porch with a pound of home-made butter or a pot of jam hidden under her apron.

'Don't let Cadwaladr know I gave you this,' she would whisper. 'Hide it in the cupboard.'

They began to invite me to their house for meals and I thought it surly to refuse what seemed such disinterested kindness.

Cadwaladr was the island postman and Monday was his day for collecting mail from the post office on the mainland. One day I went up the mountain with Nans to watch the boat on its outward crossing of the Sound.

I had been at the launching of this boat, which Cadwaladr had just fitted with a motor for the first time. It had been lashed on to a truck and pulled down to the sea, with Siani swinging monkey-like on a shaft. On our way down the steep slip to the beach, the truck took charge and almost over-ran Cadwaladr's eldest son, who was holding the shaft. We had gone mackerel-fishing as a christening for the engine.

The soft earth was riddled with shearwater burrows. From its nest we took a chick, an awkward creature covered with grey down; and were careful to keep our hands out of reach of its stabbing beak. The children took it in turns to nurse the baby bird, while their mother watched over her men far away.

10

In the evening, a thick fog rolled in, and Nans said: 'I don't think they can come home; but you can go to the Cafn just in case the boat is there.'

On my way past Clogwyn, I saw Sarah and her son Samson. The young man, with wide-open mouth and blackened teeth, blond and fresh-complexioned, held out to me a tiny birdcage picked up on the beach.

The bay was invisible, and heavy swell was running on the rocks at the entrance to the anchorage. The foghorn blew at intervals.

11

Iron, cold iron, is a deathly metal. The sea soon rusts and eats it away. A thick-linked anchor chain coils among the rocks of the Cafn; salt-bitten, repulsive as an unearthed corpse.

There is fog at the edge of the tide, sad and cold, ancient and out of time. The boat will not come back tonight. The swell breaks over the half-submerged rocks at the entrance; and the women who have waited and the women who will wait for men to come over the waves, are round me in the darkness of the boat-house. The sea eats and rusts their hearts away as it rots the links of the chain. At twilight I am far from warm-blooded contacts; chilled by an in-human world of shade. There are gulfs of fog between me and other mortals. It is as if life-blood had been turned to water. All is shadow, the suggestion of substance; an elusive hint of grey watchers among grey stone.

I have seen her on other nights when we have been returning over the sea, the shrouded figure standing motionless in a corner of the cliff: high on the mountainside over the white, the wine dark red, the mussel blue ramparts. She is not this or that familiar woman of the island, but a symbol. Monumental in patience, the woman watches the Sound. She stands on the headland, with mist drifting through her hair. Small feathers float past: on the ground are claws and fleshless wafer-thin skulls of birds. Far below, seafowl wheel and mourn over blocks of orange crag at the mountain foot.

This is a woman of the island: shawled in garments like a nun's, with face almost yellow in pallor; her grey eyes large and clear, black-lashed. Over them arch thick-haired brows that meet at the root of the primitive nose. Her mouth is half-open like an animal's, grinning in the truculent way of a fawning dog. She has the face of one haunted by the imminence of death, predicting that she will be a corpse within these next three years. Indeed, looking at her with pity and anguish, we can see that shadow darkening over her; but however weak in health, strength of custom and the power of love draw her feet up the hill path through the bracken to the place where she has the extent of water between the isle and the mainland.

She looks to have the two sights when she crouches, wide-open eyed, weary with experience, hurts, obscure questionings, suffering the thin rain to fall on to the night of her grief-puckered brows.

She watches her husband's boat and is satisfied when it reaches the black rock in safety.

Some things she sees of which she does not speak; tissues of the past still stream upon the air before her. The wide gaze of grey eyes under black arched brows. She sees without the need of sight.

A vessel throws back white foam, a full-rigged barque leans her sails to the hidden levels of the reef. Figures float water-like on her decks, over a cargo of oysters in the hold. They gesture with the disillusioned gestures of the drowned, floating gently, purged of flesh, on the deck over the oyster-shells. Under the deck, shells contain oysters, and in some the irritant pearl.

In this present of her vision (for I have said elsewhere that past and future merge into the living moment on and about this sea-rock) the boat returns; figment of tissue, integrating, falling apart, her holds empty. The oysters have returned to their bed. Sold to the red-faced, roystering merchants of a seaport on the coast of England. The crew lurches, men and women, dizzy on the salt-caked decks. They are up to the gills in drink. The white sails lean, full as bladders; the white sails shiver and slap dead as shrouds about the vessel's body. Waves like mountain ranges rise to ruin her. The drunken sailors sucking the salt spray, lip-licking it down on gusts of laughter, have lost their wits so that they overshoot the anchorage and are in the open sea. The ship wallows, drunk as her crew. Staggering, her patient timbers surprised, she yaws, steadies, lifts, and sinks into nightmare. Black torrents pour over her bows. With a sigh, her sails betray her, and she capsizes into the hurrying impatient surf. The sea is full of faces, and it is a sea of faces, the incredulous fixed faces of the doomed. This is the death by drowning: not for me; for him, for you: but not for me. The faces go down, and the arms; the disbelieving eyes begin to understand. One woman in a cotton skirt hooped in a bell shape of wire, floats in to the shore, still breathing, one breather to remember a drunken voyage; one inherited memory to fill a woman's sight when she sits in the summer rain.

12

The watercrock in the dairy was empty so I picked up the two buckets and went to the well at the foot of the mountain.

Shutting the heavy iron gate behind me, I took up the buckets. By the wall, just inside the mountain and near the upper end of the graveyard, was sitting a young rabbit. It was crouched perfectly motionless, with its eyes open unblinking. It was strange for a rabbit to be sitting dead in that position. You see, I took it for granted that it was dead. One of the farm dogs was with me but he took no notice of the creature. I went up to it, grasped it by the ears and shook it backwards and forwards. The coldness of its ears almost numbed my fingers so that I shuddered and relaxed my hold. I did not like to see it sitting crouched in such a way when it was dead. Should I take it back for the pot?

I went up to the well, filled my buckets, and returned to the gate. The rabbit still sat there. I turned away. There was a small sound: the rabbit had vanished.

When they heard my story in the house, they said I must have met with one of the saints in animal shape. And later in the day, a rabbit was seen sitting on one of the tombs in the churchyard.

13

From the north end, cries and curses came through drifting fog.

Nans and Tudur were putting a heifer to the bull. Mist swirled in spirals through the arched gateways of the stackyard. Nans, with a grey coat over her head, the sleeves tied under her chin, stood white and trembling in the dense air. Her black brows made one line over the haunted eyes. She was screaming in every passionate note to Tudur; that he must run for safety, that he would be killed. He answered with equal violence, begging, ordering her to climb the gate into the field. Both of them were frantic with the thought that the other might be injured.

With sticks and stones in our hands, we ran shouting along the walls. Siani, scarlet with excitement under freckles and sunburn, danced on the corrugated iron roof of the woodshed in nailed boots, adding her demon cries to the general uproar.

Only the heifer and the bull kept comparatively calm; quietly taking themselves off into the fog; to reappear again suddenly as flat grey shapes, the bull poised thrusting on the heifer's back.

The act of copulation over, the bull was driven back to the meadow at the point of a pitchfork. The beast made huge by fog passed close to us, clouded as if running in his own furious breath.

The children sang paeans of triumph; even when they were in bed they continued to shout hysterically and to chant hymns. Their savage cries blended with the sound of shearwater and foghorn.

14

It was still foggy the next morning, but by afternoon the sea had sucked up the mist. The children, the dogs, and I went along the cliffs to drive the sheep into the pens. We cleaned and doctored the sheep against maggots.

We picked mushrooms, and paddled idly in the coves, looking for brock.

The boat returned over an oily calm; she was almost across the Sound, coming in close under Ogof Pant, before we saw her. Seals were basking, wailing and sobbing; or they snorted their vast contentment of full belly, on the surface. The sea was slack and quite hushed.

An inflated red-ripe sun went behind the Wicklows, and at the last, those mountains smoked with legendary fires before the chill of night covered them.

15

Storm or calm weather O Lord: storm or calm weather. Cadwaladr tormented himself during days and nights before the great Sunday excursion of his kinsmen out of Lleyn. Storm or calm weather; in those words he spoke out of his whole nature, for this man of violent moods had no room for half measures in weather or in anything else. Let the water rave in green madness or stretch like ice to the horizon. With either he was content, for he understood the passionate tumult of waves through the undisciplined passions of his own heart; understood also the flat calms when drowned mountain ranges showed as purple stains on a glass sea. For he knew infrequently a placid hour. The half and half drove him frantic. If the weather was neither good nor bad, treacherous, erratic, then he was disturbed in his whole life, making those about him nervous and sick with tension.

The Sunday morning broke with unquestionable fairness, and was kind in the sunlight. Even the evil hawks and the predatory Little Owls were silent. What was this day that it was kept as high festival? Was it simply the royal weather, gold and blue from dawn to sunset, making of the island a place of pilgrimage? Or was it the relic of pagan festival forgotten in the brain but carried in the blood?

The men were off early to cross with the morning tide to the mainland well where the sister's sons and the distant cousins would be waiting.

Nans had gone away with Siani for a week's holiday, so I was deputising at Pant.

I set the boys to chopping a supply of wood for the oven, and in the strong heat of the lovely morning I toiled at preparing a princely dinner worthy of eight strong men.

It seemed before I had had time to turn round three times that Cadwaladr was back, saying the visitors had gone to the lighthouse and would be up to the farm directly. Next, they were standing in the churchyard across the path outside the kitchen window, looking at the abbey ruin, reading the carved names on the stone boxes. These youths reading the inscriptions, in faces and clothing did not belong to this century at all, but to the adolescent days of my grandparents, to the time of the first bicycle; for they were in stiffly uncomfortable suits, high rigid collars, and cloth caps. Young ploughmen, dairy hands; starched into such a Sabbath respectability that they had lost the earthy quality of everyday. Cadwaladr, grinning broadly, showed them with pride the wonders of the island.

The heavy iron pot with its hunk of roasted meat and potatoes was taken from the oven and put in the middle of the table. As the cousins and nephews filed in, removing their caps as if entering a church, they cast bashful glances at me. The boys were put to eat alone in the parlour, for there was insufficient room at the kitchen table. Nobody spoke. We almost choked with anxiety not to choke, not to draw attention to ourselves. There was a champing of jaws, scraping of knives and forks. The lads giggled in the safety of the parlour. Smiling, we looked at one another. Sometimes, there came a splutter from the lads, and a burst of wild laughter. They found it hard to bear the unnatural silence in which we ate.

'A little more, Dafydd? More, Sion?'

Cadwaladr hovers his knife over the meat. He is in a flannel shirt grey-and-white striped under his best waistcoat. His face is smoothed of care, beautiful in its golden seal transparency of skin. Benignant, patriarchal face, and hair iron-grey at the temples. A holy priest, a devil, or father of a line of strong-thewed men.

He is a man with a knife, blindly hacking to appease his consuming rage. A demon with a knout, his arm always raised to strike; a man of fire and thundercloud. A man of smouldering despairs; a thoughtful, calm-browed scholar reading a book of foreign travels. At times, a mischievous boy looking out of his middle age. Sly and daring, critical of life.

He is all these and more.

Roast and vegetables were finished. Dishes of baked pudding and pastry followed. Through the door of the oven fierce heat struck my back.

'Nice pictures you've got, Cadwaladr,' said Sion. Everyone gazed up at the two framed photographs of biscuits.

'Makes your mouth water, doesn't it?' said Dafydd.

You are gipsy-dark, you men from the opposite coast, with oval heads and black bashful eyes. You do not belong to this century; you posed long ago in front of sham columns against a backcloth of improbable trees and summer clouds, with one hand on the rail of an insubstantial gilt chair, the other with spread fingers on an outthrust hip. You are men from an album known in childhood; and yet you are living and are my contemporaries.

The boys in the parlour spluttered and giggled.

By the middle of the afternoon the tide was right for taking the cousins back to the other side. When the cakes had been taken out of the oven and the black pot full of fish coated with butter had been put in to bake for our supper, I ran after the men to the Cafn, for

Cadwaladr had asked me if I would care to drink at the pilgrims' well.

Calm: two lighthouses; one in air, one in water. From the land-anchored roots another lay deep in the sea, undistorted, gay in red and white blocks of colour.

We gently slid out over the motionless underworld, where forests of giant weed stood untremulous on the rock floor. Fleets of small fishes shot between the branches of this forest land, and I shifted my weight to feel the boat respond and sway gently on the fat sea. It held us on its yielding breast.

From the other side of Pen Clogwyn came the sound of engines. Two boats with shining outboards dashed the sprays apart. Brigands, sea robbers, stood in them laughing. They hailed us loudly, drunk with adventure and the glitter and joy of the day. They stood close-packed in the trough of the divided sea and laughed in their teeth. Our response was more sober, for we were curious as to who they were and what brought them here to our island.

What was this day that it should have been chosen out of all the summer to be a time of friendly invasion? Strangers roamed the mountainside. The rusty bell in the chapel porch clapped and wheezed, a pathetic cracked sound, as lads leapt up and down on the stiff chain. The harmonium squealed. For one day, the abnormal came to us. We saw men from the outer world but because they too came from lonely farms they were not actually so very different from us. To them, we were fantastic creatures to be reverenced and humoured as sea-dogs.

Perhaps this was the relic of pagan festival purged of ritual and blood sacrifice, which the dry brain had forgotten but the heart remembered. Half way across the Sound the young men produced sandwiches and handed them round; we three of the island did not eat, but glanced at one another, affronted at this reflection on our hospitality.

One of the young men was ill, and each time he vomited he solemnly took off his cap and handed it to his cousin. Then he leaned over the gunwale and was sick without losing anything of stiff Victorian decorum.

At the sea-foot below the well we leapt ashore. Owain stayed aboard to keep the boat from going on the rocks, for there is no anchorage here.

We had been watched as we came over by people sitting on the grass above the cliff. Another legend must that day have sprung up about the doings of the islandmen. Climbing the steep path, we were exultant, squeezing the last sweet drop from life.

'Drink, drink, everyone in his turn,' cried Cadwaladr.

The well was a miracle of clear water, cold, cold. It was deep and from its depths sprung clear water weeds. I let the others drink first; after they had risen and turned their faces towards the sea, I knelt on the smooth ledge and put my lips to the mirror, and wished with the belief of my heart in the efficacy of water. Think of the wells over which the human heart wishes, and wishing sighs, for it is then the body understands its loneliness, thwarted desires, impossible desires.

It is the heart craving happiness, only simple happiness which will hurt no one, craving a contentment that one cannot hold for ever. They travelled from well to well also, those who made me centuries ago. They drank from the clear water spring, the fountain of creation. Perhaps they also wished for contentment, with the superstition which endures through time.

Beloved Paul: by star and moon, sun and tempest, I sent thoughts to you with a bird call crying, come back, return to me.

The water was limpid, simple as the blue height of sky. But the island, the island, was the legendary rock, the magnet of our blood. For an instant forgetting the reality in dream I saw it as an unattainable, nameless vision. Going back through troughs and rainbow sprays, nobody in the world seemed more fortunate than I, for this was life and colour and movement under the sun. With the power of a believed-in wish behind me, and the length of a summer evening before. There was no time to wonder then as to why out of all impossible desires, my heart had instinctively asked just that: the return of the beloved who was far, impossibly far in distance. Now, as I write with him seated nearby, there is an unearthly bond of which he is unaware, between the man and the well in which I conjured his return.

As we slipped through the flat water of the Cafn towards the warm land, we saw the invaders, the mainland men, coming down from the lighthouse.

After tea, as I shook the table cloth at the back door, the bell began

68

to toll. Twm was doing the honours of the island to the strangers. They went up the mountain, which on this golden evening faced the west without a shadow on its brow. All this time Cadwaladr was wandering distractedly about the house, opening cupboards, looking in drawers, murmuring the one word: candles. I wondered what he could want with candles on a high summer evening when the house was heavy with sunlight.

He found some at last and asked me if I would care to explore Ogof Cerrig Llwydion near the mountain-top in the east.

He was like an animated boulder, a moving block, as he moved before the background of his world of snaking currents and distant hills: when he paused to talk, leaning upon his stick his feet were planted in the strong earth and grew there.

He is of the sea and mountain: they are his strength. With difficulty we found the cave in the steep declivity of crumbling earth and massive stones. Through a low entrance we went into a high-vaulted chamber which was black as night at its further end. Lighting our candles, we looked into this corner and saw how above slimy boulders the cavern ascended, twisting into the core of the mountain.

Climbing, the candlelight dim and yellow in the foul air, I feel the weight of the ground pressing on me. Rock and earth tunnel: thick vapour given off by graveyard soil. The walls ascend, lost in bluish vapours. It is more than I can bear, this moving into the womb of a hill.

Outside is the sun and an evening world. Living birds circle the yellow-lichened cliffs.

Could I be sure of remaining conscious with power to enjoy the sight of the earth, though I should be an unidentifiable spark, how much less agony my days would hold, but without agony, wild exaltation would also vanish. If I had a thousand years in which to learn the secrets of the sea, the force of my desire would become lost in the thought of eternity. Though tomorrow may be nothing to me: I nothing to tomorrow, today is mine.

The craft of the sea-robbers were racing for home side by side under the shadow of the mountain.

We followed the breastwork along the summit. Down to St. David's Head the Pembroke coast was clear, and the hills of Ireland were sombre in the west. Reaching the lighthouse at sunset we took supper with the keepers, a meal of salted beef and strong tea.

It was quite dark when we got back to the farm. The children were round the table, feasting out of the black pot of baked fish which was scarcely visible under a thick crust of bright butter. The boys' faces as they looked up were polished and glowing from lamplight on sunburnt flesh. To them also it had been a rare holiday for they had been able to show others their private mysteries.

Outside the chapel, the cracked bell hung motionless. The night-spirits of the island moved in from the ocean: shearwater after shearwater cackled and laughed until the air was evil, until there was left no memory of the day's festivity.

16

A large dark object was travelling parallel to the west coast, and I wondered whether it was an empty boat. Thinking it possible that I might have been the first to see it, I decided to go to Pant to tell them there was something adrift; but before I was ready, there came a knock at the door. Tudur stood outside.

'Have you seen the raft?'

'A raft, is it? Not a boat?'

'No, a raft. We had one before. My father and Owain have gone out for it.'

Siani came to watch the drama. Tudur went out on to the cliffs. The raft was travelling fast on the ebb towards the islet.

Cadwaladr seemed to be a long time coming round the south end. We heard the pop pop of a motor-boat engine coming from the north, and out of the shelter of the cliff came a boat travelling fast, followed by another a little way behind. Dai Penmon was in the first boat, Jacob was in the second. Instead of going against the tide to meet the raft, they had gone with the ebb right round the island to catch up with their prize.

Cadwaladr was coming up the fields, with bowed head.

'Had to give it up,' he said. 'The engine wouldn't start because of a dirty plug. Anyway, the others were out before me; had the start of me.'

He had sent Owain the cliff way to the Cafn while he went round the island, so as not to arouse suspicion; for if they had gone together, everyone would have guessed they were putting out to sea.

But Jacob had passed him, hurrying, and saying nothing of his errand; and Dai's and Jacob's boats were out already when he reached the anchorage.

'If I could have got the engine running,' he said. 'We'd have gone against the ebb to meet the raft as she came round from the west side; with the engine dead against us, we could have had no chance in such a sea.'

'I hope Dai gets the raft since we didn't,' said Nans.

Dai's boat was like a shining skimmer, dipping through the grey, black-streaked water. At times, the sun gleamed on Dai's back, and by that we could tell he was soaked in brine.

The raft was almost on the rocks of the islet by now, but the boats were able to circle her. One of them took her in tow. The sea was so dirty in the ebb that sometimes Dai's craft was lost to us; but then again it rose gallantly riding the swell. Time and again the raft had to be abandoned, the fishing boat being too small and light to take the weight of it against the drag of the sea. The two fishers began to treat it like a monstrous beast. They played it, circling, drawing away at full speed; returning again to the battle.

They were at it for about four hours, until the trophy was in the Cafn at last. The men were coated in salt.

Having marvelled less at the competition of man against the sea than at man against man in the matter of going out secretly for booty, made me think that private tunnels should be dug from each farm to the anchorage so that a man might be down and away with nobody the wiser for his going.

17

We went over to the mainland to pick blackberries.

We wandered through the heart of Lleyn, drifting idly in the day's dry heat. We were wearing our sea clothes under a sun burning from a clear sky, which caused us extreme discomfort, for we were out of touch with the land, unsure of ourselves away from the sea and the sea-rock. Everyone stared at us, marvelling at the extravagant raggedness of Cadwaladr, at Owain's long-faced head with its madness-inspired eyes. Stiff with salt, his hair was bleached almost white. His wild features and disordered hair suggested a prophetic fury.

We trespassed over the pasture of half the farms in the peninsula: climbing trees and banks and barbed wire.

Alien land.

Furtively yet defiantly, we gathered berries. In this open country lying bare under the afternoon glare, there is almost no woodland, but towards the coast stands a grove of pale-trunked trees with wind-forced branches. The road lies under the arch in cold shadow. Prisoners of war were at work in a cornfield near the grove. Smooth grey-green trunks rise from the soil, rooted in pools of shadow. Through boughs and leaves runs a tremor of small sound. To look at the powerful boles after the nakedness of the island is like seeing trees for the first time.

They are immensely alive, these trunks that have thrust upwards from the soil and are in their highest boughs speaking with the air.

Children, dwarfed by the grove, play in and out of sun patches near the walls of a farmyard breathing decay and abandonment to ruin. Nettles have overgrown rusted machinery in forgotten corners.

There are secrets in this wood.

Human life has gone from the buildings; human life has become faded or killed; the trees have closed round the reason of its going. Trying to imagine myself to be the child Siani coming to the mainland for the first time and seeing trees with fresh eyes, their uneasy shadows, life, weight, power to burst from the ground; they seemed to be monstrous and abnormal growths, fit for ritual worship.

We went down to the white sands that lay, pale and gleaming with more than common lightness of shores, against a sea and sky of equal purity and blue depth. The levels, sand, sea, and sky had horizontal perfection as though line upon line lay from the roots of the earth to the black zenith, and uniting them, crossing them vertically, bathers stood in groups along the brim of the sea.

A naked boy rode a grey horse where the waves crisped and spread, becoming lost in the hard shore. The horse was grey-dappled, its hocks black.

Sand squeaked under the tread like dry powder snow after a heavy frost has raised a crust from the earth.

We went through a maze of fields until we came to a wet copse from the bottom of which rose the high wall of a bridge. Climbing on to the roadway we set out for the bay in the face of increasing wind from the sou' west.

A strong swell was breaking on the beach. Under the lee of Cadwaladr's boat, we ate our sandwiches. Some distance off, the other island boats had just come in. Stewart and his dog sat beside the dinghy at the water's edge; there was nobody else about but the thin lonely man, the thin unhappy dog. Stewart sat with bowed head looking at the sand.

The wind increases.

Coal, the provision box, the tin of blackberries, were placed beside the oars and we slowly moved the boat till it rode the sea. The swell almost threw the boat on to the sands again.

As our ties with the land snapped, a grim world closed round us. In the space of a few moments the bay was swept with wild rains. Drenched and blinded, we could see nothing ahead. An extraordinary sensation filled the air. The sea was black and silver, gleaming where light fell on the waves, dark as death in the hollows. Mist shrouded the headlands. We and our boat were details in an eighteenth-century engraving. My heart was shaken by this unwholesome entry into another period of time, for I did not belong to this steely seascape. I had often looked through pictures into this past time: at cold seas, dim mountains, water spouts, and had thought they belonged to the engraver's tool, that there had never been in nature so grey and austere a scene. This seemed to be the mirage of the past; Cadwaladr crouched at the tiller, his eyes glaring out from under the peaked cap. He and Owain had bare legs and feet; their trousers were rolled high up their thighs. Owain knelt in the bows, lashing the heavy oars together so that they should remain firm as the boat rolled sideways.

There was so much rain and spray that I could not see where we were going. The headland was steel, and the hanging clouds.

A herd of horses plunges at the entrance to the Sound. We dare their hooves and burst into the passage between mainland and island. From the north-east the rock stands lost in its own melancholy shadow.

No landing place, no habitation. It seems so far away behind its shrouds of bleak rain. Cadwaladr accelerates the engine and the boat smacks the water. Against our speed, waves break over the bows to drench us in flying spray. Salt trickles down my face and into my mouth. Now visible on the back of a wave, now lost in a trough, Jacob rides the seas ahead of us.

You who are in the safety of the world, can you guess what this going home means to the islander?

We search out one another's forms across the desert of water, and smile into one another's eyes.

'Myfanwy told me we would have a bad passage home tonight,' I say to Cadwaladr. 'How could she know in this morning's fine weather that it would be stormy tonight?'

Cadwaladr smiles subtly. 'I know why she said that,' he answers.
'Why?'

'Never mind now. I'll tell you when we land.' With one eye open against the stinging spray I see the island coming nearer. Then it disappears in a smother of spray; comes again to sight.

Now Cadwaladr had one of his sudden inspirations. Speaking curtly, in a tone not to be questioned, he ordered the young Tudur to put on an ancient overcoat that had been lying over the engine-casing; told him to stand up with arms outstretched. Thus he hoped by using his son as a mast and the old coat as a sail, to steal a small advantage from favourable wind.

We leave the Sound and pass along the back of the mountain in the dusk. Squalls and gusts sweep the gullies. We pass through chaotic waters, now lifted up, pushed forward by giant hands, now sucked to one side by the sea monster that would capsize us.

As we come towards the Cafn, Cadwaladr puts the engine at half speed. We lift our mackerel lines out of the water at the bottom of the boat. Wet as we are we fish for supper as darkness falls; up to the black rocks of the south end, round under the lighthouse, down towards the night of Pen Clogwyn. The mackerel thump their lives out on the bottom of a box. In the gloom of the anchorage the children wait for us, and the island breathes of summer even in this night, this rain.

I accompanied Cadwaladr to the lighthouse through a spanking wind. We stood in the overheated kitchen which was starkly clean; our clothes dripped dismally. Cadwaladr gave the keepers the mainland news, gesturing with customary wildness. Letters fell from his hands about the floor.

Walking home under the dazzle and dark of the beam, he suddenly asked, 'Do you know why Myfanwy said we would have a bad crossing tonight?'

'No.'

'Because of the berries,' he said. 'They are stolen fruits, don't you see? That was our punishment, the storm we came through.'

He did not tell me that he had not dared to explain Myfanwy's words when we were on the water lest he tempt providence, but I understood.

'There was another time when the same thing happened,' he went on. 'We had been to the white sands that time, too. Owain and the eldest girl were with me in the boat, and we had picked pounds and pounds of blackberries. A cruel storm struck us just as we left the shelter of the mainland. That night I sweated blood. I tell you, it was a test of the last ounce in me.'

'You got back safely that night?'

'Yes,' he said, 'but those mountains of water! And we could not get round the headland against the tide, no matter how we tried to trick our way between the waves. We made for Ogof Hir, letting the tide rip us along towards the south. Even then, it was a pull for our very lives to make the shelter of the cove. After that, it took us two days to drag the boat up the clay on to the top of the cliff.'

I followed my own thoughts in the pattern of the night.

A light showed in the kitchen of Stewart's house. The foxy dog gave his alarm from a chain at the back door, saying as plain as human speech, this is an unhappy house I guard.

Cadwaladr said, 'There's a letter for Twm.' He vanished through a gap in the hedge.

I continued on my way alone, past the deserted cottage where a boat-builder had once lived; having found it a convenient hide-out whence he could be free of the wife and many children he had left on the opposite coast; whistling, whittling, selfishly happy; smoothing a plank or the rib of a boat.

I was sleepy and confused in my thoughts. Perhaps a man had not lived there after all, but an old woman given over entirely to melancholy. She was tainted with insanity on the female side, and had been overtaken by a black and melancholy horror of the sea. She had gone over the hill for the last time, picking sticks for the fire, bundling them together in a coarse sacking apron. When she was found at the foot of the deepest gully, the seabirds had long been crying her name. Her eyes were gone and her flesh had been ravished; many birds keened her. Perhaps she had fallen, they say, or maybe she had thrown herself down there. It did not matter how or why now she had no problems.

Melancholy had always run in the family. Look at Sarah, they would say; her mouth, isn't it always open on a gasp of despair? It is the sea that does it; being too big.

18

The two-headed serpent breeds something fearful between shore and shore; a secret which only the grinning dogfish understand.

'Is the bull out in the open yard?' they are always crying. The bull rushes past the high crosses, now streaming tall with light, then dark, then with radiant light.

Nihil ad vos? O viatores omnes, cries the table of stone in the churchyard. O stone, stone dweller in this western burial ground, how you pierce us with words. Who were you before you were worm and through worm, dust, that you have power to move us with words carved on your gravestone? It is nothing to you, all ye who pass by? There are few passers-by on this piece of earth; but the cry from your stone lips is in our understanding. Intuemini et videte. I have spent long hours looking into my heart.

An sit dolor par dolori meo. The world is in ashes of sorrow. Each one of us is forced to bear the cross. Sicherlich, du hast deins auch. Nihil ad vos? O viatores omnes. Intuemini et videte an sit dolor par dolori meo, qui factus est mihi.

They get into our skins after they have shed theirs, the old people.

Beneath the upturned boat that houses them, the farmyard hens stir in sleep. The children's faces, eager in the lamplight, glance up as I pass the window.

Above the tide-mark, among a chaos of boulders, lay a petrified, tonsured monk with his robe huddled on high shoulders, the stone face pressed into a rock pillow. When I pointed him out to the children of Pant, they averted their eyes and were uncomfortable until we had moved further along the shore, but Tudur looked back once or twice at the sea-carven priest.

19

One day, during that first long summer, in a restless mood, I explored the rocks near the north end; peering into dense forests of weed that gripped the smooth slopes rising from the seabed. Silver and gold lichens enamelled a pool; hard blue mussels; soft anemones; mounds of flesh stretched nervous tentacles for food. Acorn barnacles; limpets; and when I put my finger on the tentacles of the anemone they shut themselves, the blue frill closing on to the wine-dark heart. With my fingernail I scraped the crust, the stone-hard patina of rockpools. The incoming tide sucked fronds under the rocks and then flung them out like widespread fingers on the swell.

Along the sea-margin, oystercatchers screamed from orange bills. A light wind ruffled the peacock fan of the waves. Heat shook the horizon.

20

I escaped from the house and ran to join the children who were looking over the lambs for maggots. It was sultry weather with a dull swell breaking on the shore. We drove the sheep before us along the headland and into the pens, all without a dog, so we had to do our own running. Those sheep that were maggoty were lying away from their fellows in sheltered places under the banks. When Owain had tracked one down he walked quietly along the other side of the bank, out of sight of the sheep. He then threw himself over, and held the struggling animal until Tudur came with the shears and the lotion. Owain cut away the infected fleece and where the maggots had burrowed into the flesh, cleansed and disinfected the wound.

I spent a long time on the mountain looking out to sea. The slopes were withered and polished by the sun, and in bare places I had to sit down and slide, for I was wearing old leather slippers so badly broken that they had to be fastened to my feet with strips of cloth.

21

It was early morning, one of those rare beginnings when the sea is calm, milk-blue and smooth; a morning of blue and gold with a heavy dew cold as frost. I was out in the west fields picking mushrooms for the men to take over to the mainland; my mind as blank and peaceful as the water, when a sudden uproar arose, one of those events that delighted us always; drama and the breaking of too-quiet an existence was eagerly awaited. For it is an unspoken tradition on the island that scandal and extravagant deeds are our meat and drink. It ran like fire through grass; the Mariner's wife's water had broken; she would give birth at any time, now!

The Ancient Mariner had drowsed ten years of his life away since coming to the island; lying asleep in springtime in a field corner while his horse stood patiently at the plough, or hiding himself in the village when he went over to do the shopping. He usually hid in a corner where he could read in peace until, rousing himself just as the boat was leaving the beach, he would dash from between the pub and the churchyard, waving his book and shouting to his neighbours to wait for him.

The Mariner's wife was expecting her third child. She had steadfastly refused to go ashore until the last possible moment, since she was preoccupied at that time in rearing a large brood of chicks under an incubator. A few nights before she went away, the light went out and she had no matches in the house with which to relight the lamp. Her husband was fast asleep, for lazy living kept him constantly fatigued; and she knew he would be savage for days if she dared to disturb him. It was a warm easy night; so she set out for the lighthouse wearing only a nightdress. She knew one man at least would be on duty in the tower. In the living quarters, two men were asleep, and she could see the third man's shadow moving around the lantern. She climbed the stone stairs of the tower, and came out quietly at the top of the steep stairhead. The poor man,

80

believing himself to be the only person awake at that time of night, and not having heard her coming, bellowed with fear, thinking she was a ghost.

'Can you lend me a match?' she asked, as if it were the most natural thing in the world for a pregnant woman to come on such an errand.

Now, these few days later, her time came upon her in the middle of the afternoon, but even then she kept calm. The other islanders accompanied her to the anchorage; she steadfastly refused to be carried on any sort of litter; but when the pains came on with particular violence, she lay by the roadside groaning and writhing like a cow in calf, to the amusement of the children. She was wearing a thin cotton dress and no coat though the day had turned out cold.

In the middle of the Sound, she gave birth to a son. Her husband whipped out his gutting-knife for the purpose of cutting the umbilical cord, but was stopped by Cadwaladr just in time.

She returned to the island three weeks later; and helped the men to push the boat out from the beach, wading waist-high in the sea.

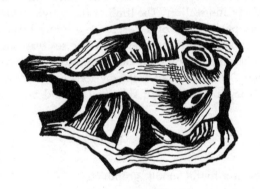

22

After a night of storm, through the drowned windows I saw Cadwaladr going down to the Cafn, where the boats were awash. The high spring tide had rushed up between the rocks and had dragged the anchor chains all ways, until they were hopelessly entangled. Side ropes had snapped, and several boats were in danger of being carried out to sea. There was water up to the level of the turf round the storehouse, and Dai Penmon had to wade waist-high to rescue his fishing boat. In the evening, at the top of the tide, everyone was called out; men, women, and children, to help bring up the boats to the top of the Cafn. The black cattle boat and the island boat had to be drawn up by winch over the shore which by this time was littered with driftwood.

A straw mattress partly submerged, went past, followed by other flotsam of a wreck: blocks of seasoned oak, chip strawberry baskets stained with juice, sticks of salt-spoiled celery still in bundles, a tin of Chat Noir boot polish on the lid of which was the picture of a black cat for bad luck. A five-foot rule. Two sailor's jerseys, the cuff of a naval jacket the braid of which was hoary with salt, a red pom-pom, a thick candle-end of glittering wax, scrubbing brushes, a sea boot, fibre mats. A short distance off-shore, I imagined there to be a bloated leg sticking like a rotten green post from a mass of bladder-wrack.

And the sea shall give up its dead to feed its chickens. O thou drowned mariners!

The sounding-board of the cliff struck out impersonal echoes of bird-cry and seal-cry. The limb or the bough (whichever it may have been) putrid flesh of a corpse or a living branch of apple, thrust like an accusation into the light. The sea was oil, chopped, raging, treacherous. Shadows ran along the waves, dark red, darker than the water. Detaching itself from my feet, my shadow flew away to the horizon, and like a bird skimmed up and down the wave-troughs.

23

Nans in a fretful mood, grumbled.

'There is nothing to eat for supper.'

It was Sunday, so there could be no question of fishing from a boat; through the summer fog Cadwaladr and I went to the rocks with heavy poles for the catching of rock-fish. Our hair hung in elf-locks, clammy and sticky in the damp air. The idea seemed to be that God could see you fishing from a boat, but not from a secret niche.

Almost at once, a fish took the morsel of soft crab and threshed up, a flash of life against the dead mist.

Other men in western isles must have been crouching as we were crouched, on ledges a few feet above the sea, with lines going down into deep water; weathered men and children, sitting in the shadow of the rocks, baiting hooks for bright-scaled fish.

Oysterfishers, rock-fishers, dour, heavily bearded, clothed in home-spun, thick sea jerseys, tall hats. One man with a spade beard wears a tam-o'-shanter. An old woman in whalebone and hoop sits in the lee of a boat whose paint has faded to grape-bloom and dim pink. Her wrinkled, hard-lined face is framed by a starched cap under a black straw bonnet.

A strong swell was running past, from which a seal watched us. Almost asleep in the stone bay, I let the sprit hang too far over the water, so that the line became fouled in the weeds. Climbing slowly backwards, I heaved at the line, until it came free at last. As the mist cleared, I saw several seals not far from us; and our unsuccessful fishing was explained. A black bull seal, the biggest one I ever saw, lay basking. His body showed green, blue, black.

North-eastwards, we could see a little of the mountain and the entrance to the Sound. Scuds of rain swept up the slopes and blowing against the run of the waves, lifted white clouds of spray high in the air and bore them across the entrance to the bay.

Suddenly, my line tautened, dragging the heavy sprit downwards. A bronze rock-fish with gaping mouth lashed from the sea with the sun flashing on its bronze-copper casing, its bright-armoured scales, and with the rising of the fish we began to talk for the first time freely; constraint falling from us, we made our first overtures at friendship.

Cadwaladr in the immobility of his pose, was part of the cliff against which he leant.

'I don't care whether I see other people or not,' he said. 'They don't mean much to me; but the wife gets sick of it here, sometimes —the women always do. There's a bit too much adventure here for them; they don't like the strain of not having a doctor at hand for the children. I remember, when one of ours fell sick, Nans was nearly out of her mind for days.'

We fished for a while in silence, then he went on:

'Unless the man and the woman pull together in this life, there's bound to be trouble; and it's no use for a woman to try living here on her .own, because she's just a liability to everyone.'

Soon we had a sackful of rock-fish whose jade and sensuous lips smiled even in death. Of every imaginable shade, from reddish-black to bronze and turquoise and yellow, fat and immaculately scaled, they proved to be difficult to prepare for cooking. Owain instructed me in this as in so much else during my earliest days on the island. Placing a heavy board on the slate slab in the dairy he nailed the fish to it by the head and with a pair of pliers ripped off the skin in one piece from gills to tail, revealing firm and faintly green flesh.

24

With a great cry, Sarah's geese flew away; heads to the wind, they flew towards the sunset, winging strongly.

'Sarah's geese have flown,' they told me when we came up from fishing. So Cadwaladr was afraid his geese might be drawn by the same urge to fly into the west.

'Even if they do come back,' he said: 'they land in the coves and break their wings on the rocks.'

We went into the lower fields near the north end to find his geese and drive them up to be clipped. They were driven hissing into one of the pig sties. Cadwaladr drew out the stiff pinions and the shears bit into the quills. After they had been clipped, the birds gathered in furious debate. It gave a sense of restless insecurity, a taste of wintriness, to think of those other geese throwing themselves towards the west after the red winter sun.

Nans in a black apron and a clean dress sat at the hearth combing her thin wiry hair, with Merfyn beside her. The shape of the cross towering outside the window threw a gloomy shadow over the room.

Merfyn inhabits a macabre world of phantom horses, fiery bulls, clutching hands, the tramp of dead men's feet. During the evening, before going on duty at midnight he lays the seeds of terror, recounting fearsome adventures as we sit round a fire of crackling twigs. We sit relaxed; Cadwaladr bows his head.

'I will tell you a story of my childhood on the mainland,' said Merfyn. 'One Sunday morning I was taken by my father for a walk through the cemetery. Being head in air, I had the misfortune to fall into an open grave. I looked about; a skull lay at my feet. I played with the bones until Father came with the ladder to fetch me out. I fitted the jaws together, and scraped away the mould filling the eyeholes. I climbed up the ladder, bringing the skull with me. Father said, "Ah, I've always wanted one of those to put over the fireplace!" We took it home, but hid it from Mother's sight. Father blackleaded it until the bones shone; then he put it in the middle of the overmantel. Mother came into the room and screamed when she saw the niggered head. She cried "Out with it, out with it." I never saw it again,' finished Merfyn.

With trembling hands, he lit a cigarette, his face haunted by the inhibitions bred in the air of nonconformity.

He imagines that bears will suddenly rear out of the darkness as he flits along the narrow lane. The hands of a man he used to know, since dead, strain to reach him out of the small window near the landing of the lighthouse.

The door at the bottom of the tower opens to unseen hands. He hears deathly voices.

'Old Dai Richardson tried to grab me again last night, and there was a man in the tower last week, singing to himself about a shipwreck. Dai Richardson has been at my bedside every night, buttoning up his pants, old-fashioned seaman's trousers, and on his back a jacket with dull brass buttons.'

'Does he speak to you?' we ask.

'How do I know? As soon as he comes, I cover my head under the blankets.'

25

One of Cadwaladr's mainland cousins had a taxi for hire. One afternoon, he drew up in the village and strolled down to see the boat's engine being repaired.

Cadwaladr looked up at last, after he had finished thinking; he was restless, and gazed into the distance.

'We could go back on this tide, or we could wait until the evening,' he said. 'Would you like to come upcountry in the car?'

We drove through the resting countryside where cottages showed no life and animals were asleep in the fields. We drew up outside a small shop at a cross-roads. Inside, a gaunt woman was buying up the shop in ounces and half-ounces. The man behind the counter had a sleepy voice: flies hummed among the sugar bags. Cadwaladr, who bought a new one almost every week during the summer months, began to finger thick tweed waistcoats.

The woman whispered, 'Two ounces of yeast. An ounce of nutmeg. Half an ounce of cloves.'

Her tongue was as if overlaid with dust.

NUTMEG AND GINGER

Mother said, 'Go to the shop for me:
Ask the woman with silver fingernails
If she has nutmeg ginger cinnamon honey.'

Because of a weak remembrance,
At every step I had to repeat
The names of these spices and fragrance.

By a miracle of sweet Lord Jesus,
I memorised these four sweetnesses,
So my mother gave me two ancient pennies.

With one, I bought a liquorice bootlace,
The other I dropped behind me for luck;
Gaining by this, both good value and solace.

'Please, may I have a pound of candles?' I was thinking of the long nights torn by the cries of shearwaters.

The shopkeeper, slow-moving, gentle-faced, is said to have the secret of rooting out malignant growths common to this part of the county; and he is known as the wild wart man. His brow was thoughtful as he dropped the brass weights on to the scales and made up small packages of yeast and pepper.

Next, we went off in search of a pair of castrators. I sat on the running-board of the car, stupid with sun, by a duck-pond on which children were sailing a lopsided yacht. It could have been the birthplace of the Three-masted Schooner.

GREEN LADS OF SARN

Wind in the toy cordage
Of the little ship,
The three-master,
The whistler!

A model boat busy
On the pond waves
Commanded by
Boys of Sarn
And a deckhand
From the Java run—
Of bone and coral:
The three-master,
The over-topper!

So douce she was,
So white her shrouds.
She stepped out
Like a queen
Setting her virgin course
For a harbour beyond the Cape,
The lily-wise courser!

We kept watch
Over a minute ocean.
When the wind set sou' west
Along the Calf,
I would horn my hand
To the tiller
Of the haven-seeker!

Land roared astern,
The mountain peaks
Vanished. Sedges, waterweed,
The cliff-pond, all behind.
Before us, the world of dust-
Raddled palms on Singapore beach.

When we were small,
We owned a three-master,
Lifted anchor when we pleased,
Hoisted the mainsail
Towards the Indies
In search of gold crosses
For throats, and pearl
For the ship's keel.
She was our treasure, the
Triple-branched schooner,
The white sea-corsair!

26

During the length of that summer the bull was in a wild mood, bellowing continuously; climbing out of his field by way of the grass ramp, and galloping into the bottom field where he ranged in defiance of his empty world. I was constantly afraid that one day the unsuspecting children would meet the angry beast face to face and be gored to death.

I took the boys to Ogof Goch, where the cave walls were luminous with sunlight. We tried to salvage a long plank of new wood, carried by the tide parallel to the rock ledges; but we failed to get it.

The cove has a short, upward-sloping beach of wave-smoothed boulders. At low water, with the sun shining directly into the entrance, the wet walls are red as beet-juice and slimy with countless contracted sea-anemones. At water level the dove-coloured rock is encrusted with a lavender lichen; in faults of the cliff-face above the chasm, choughs have built their nesting-place; the cave becomes a

sounding-board of clamour and protestation when the birds discover that humans have dared to come so near their young.

At high water, under an evening sun, each stone is surrounded by its own rainbow, shaking and shimmering in ripple-disturbances.

We are blessed with private rainbows: from the mountain summit, the circle of prismatic colours is almost complete; the arch overhead and the arms going down below us into the sea.

In autumn, the Irish horizon has its broken watery bows. In winter crossings, as we plough through rain and salt spray, we have been held in the close dazzle of our own intimate rainbow, travelling the current with us.

27

Cadwaladr walked through the house to the sitting-room and returned carrying his gun. He put his hand on my shoulder, saying, 'I'm going out to shoot the sick cow, little one.'

The diseased beast in the meadow of the ruined house had been a reproach to the teeming summer. Every night it had seemed she must die before morning: every day, that she must die before nightfall. She was a woeful creature of skin-covered bones and those bones misshapen. She was kept segregated from the rest of the herd. Though I never saw her grazing, she must had fed sometimes. Otherwise, how could she have kept alive for so long? She either lay or stood with lowered head as if in a trance, or limped across the meadow dragging her rotted hindquarters. Cadwaladr said she had torn one of her legs on barbed wire during the spring. The member having become infected, poison had travelled through her whole body.

From the kitchen window I had a clear view of the cow in the field and of the man with his gun. With the weapon held behind his back, he walked up to her; she was apprehensive and hobbled away. Cadwaladr climbed the wall out on to the open mountain and went behind the hedge. He moved back and forth while the cow watched him through tangled bushes of nectar-dripping fuschias. The cow sensed that her hour had come. The man hesitated.

There was a shot, and the cow's legs went up before she fell dead on her side. Cadwaladr came round into the field and stood over the body for a long time.

Then Owain was sent into the field to dig a deep grave. Cadwaladr paced up and down anxiously, because as he said, he 'Wasn't sure where the other buggers had been buried.'

28

The highest of the churchyard crosses confronted me when I awakened and turned on to my back on the hard clothes chest beside the kitchen range.

Of what had I been thinking when I fell asleep?

'Close-fitting armour keeps out loneliness.' The headstone with a willow on it, the burrowing worm so vital, taking my life away, transforming the corpse into another organism, both will fall into decay. Who cares, who should care when a winged thistle seed drifts over the sea? There is happiness to seize, loneliness to bear.

In a colourless dawn, the windows were covered with salt spray. The sou' west wind shrieked in keyhole and chimney. Against the rocks the tide-race poured in a green flood. On the west side ran a swell from which rollers reared to break as they met the island. The wind running across the tide tore plumes from the wave-tops. We had been cut off from the mainland for a week by monstrously heavy seas.

As soon as they were dressed, the children set off for the coves in search of driftwood; so we breakfasted without them on tea, mackerel, and bread and butter.

They returned when the meal was half over, glancing eagerly in as they passed the kitchen window. With staring eyes and hair they might have been demons. Tudur held out a live lobster.

'We found it in Porth Solfach. It must have been washed up in the storm.'

'You didn't take it from a pot?' demanded his father.

'No, it was washed up on the beach.'

The lobster was put with the crabs on the dairy floor, where they sighed and blew together. The claws of the shellfish scraped the tiles in vain, hopelessly seeking for a deep rock-pool.

'We got a fourteen-foot plank too,' said Tudur, taking a ship's biscuit from the sea-crusted tin on the table.

29

At this time, the boys spent most of every day in the coves dragging driftwood above high water mark or looking for choughs' nests on the precipices.

From constant exposure, the children developed sore throats so that they could only croak when they tried to sing. Their eyes became bloodshot and watery. After they had been put to bed in the big room facing the mountain, I went up with doses of epsom salts. They were seated side by side watching the candle shadows form shapes of birds and flying fish on the wall. Half apprehensive, half hysterical, they watched me.

'Where is the jar of honey?' I demanded.

'I don't know.' Looking at one another, they burst into confession.

'It's on the top shelf in the dairy.' Laughing uneasily, they collapsed on to the pillows. When I pressed for an explanation, they told me what had happened.

'You were out fishing; and we were left to make our own tea. We wanted honey, but the jar broke on the tiles. We saved a little of it and hid it in another jar on top of the shelf.'

They were given what remained of the honey in hot water. Downstairs, their father was preparing an infusion of mint, parsley, senna pods and ground ivy; a home-made medicament of most evil smell and colour. Under protest, the children drank it.

'Go to sleep now; but first, tie your socks round your necks.'

They giggled. 'We can't; they're stinking from the sea.'

When I went downstairs, I found the lighthouse-man Merfyn standing at the kitchen table. With bulging eyes, he was watching the making of the witches' brew. At last, he could bear it no longer. With a gasp, he muttered, 'Good night; I must be off,' and fled through the doorway.

By morning, the children were almost free of fever.

30

This life is a perpetual struggle with storm. At the south end of the island, the lashing gale flung us about until we were soaked in spray. Breakers creamed and struck with fury. Our minds were dulled, our heads ached.

Merfyn was standing like a bedraggled bird at the gate leading to the lighthouse, hailing us to come in for shelter.

They were making the afternoon test on the radio telegraph.

SOS. SOS. SOS.

The room crackled with tension.

'South Bishops calling cream two-masted sailing boat drifting steadily eastwards her yard arm broken Saint David's lifeboat Saint David's lifeboat can you hear me?'

Distorted by atmospherics, the monotonous call went on.

'Here is a message about a cream two-masted . . .' Five people were aboard the yacht; two men, a woman, and two children; blown across the Irish Sea they were in imminent danger of being destroyed

on the rocks of St. Bride's Bay. The sails had been blown away; her yard arm snapped off.

At dusk, the family gathered in the chapel. We sang the hymn 'For those in peril on the sea.'

I watched the faces of the children. Though the cold house of God was at the centre of the storm the children were oblivious to everything but the novelty of being in church. The wind mingled with the wheezing of the harmonium. Cadwaladr was quite unlike himself, sitting with a clean and shaven face and an untroubled brow; his deep voice almost drowned by the shrieking of the wind and the groans of the harmonium.

We discovered that Tudur, wearing his mother's coarse apron had in our absence scrubbed the kitchen and dairy floors. Merfyn, a cloth bag containing milk bottles clutched between his knees, was watching the work with a sarcastic smile.

The wind must surely have been tired of howling round the house.

31

Cadwaladr was big with grief and comedy like any ancient hero. Twisted and corrupt, with bitter roots, he stood four-square on field and rock. Harsh and dogmatic, no mood of Celtic yearning ever touched him. His existence was primitive, and passionate with rage and self-inflicted torment. He was spawned of the sea: thrown up on a weed-hung wave, with horned shells twisted in his black hair; as if the ocean had given him up to live on land for a time, and would eventually draw him back into the foaming tideway. Yet, for all that, his savagery was shot through with tenderness of such poetry as to sometimes surprise. He could be cunningly aware of the feelings of others; he could show a grudging admiration of other men if they were tough-fibred and had proved themselves. He was primitive and self-reliant, with the qualities of an old race driven back on itself along the sea-margin. He was not degenerate through this inversion, but had built from solitude a front of audacious courage and contempt for death. There were many weak places in his armour; times of paralysing depression when he would sit for long periods head in arms, closed away from the world; times when he might be plotting a subtle devilry or be gripped by the torment of remorse.

In a wild mood, he would wander the mountainside; his heart's restlessness denying him peace; but then, no man is so contented with life that he does not at times grow eager to break with the sameness of his days, to seek green immortality in troughs of the tideway.

The wife who sits at home before the red hearth does not know with what endurance he faces danger in paths of exile.

A seabird in its breast shakes out its wings; lifts its feet from the ledge of his heart; flies out with the ebb and returns on the strength of the flood-tide that pours into the seal caves, over the jasper shore. It leaves its shadows on the waters that surround land, follows the curve of the earth, and comes back to its nest in his heart.

This bird, not to be denied, torments and heals the heart of him who now by the pole star, now by the sun at noon, guides his craft over whale-paths.

He is handing on to me the living tradition of the island's past that is the present moulding the future.

He leads me to the stone basins on the eastern escarpment into which pure water wells up; to the home of mammoth crabs in the islet to the westward; talks of winds and tides; shows me the stone compass near the Cafn. Laying open the mysteries and qualities of the island, he pleads like Caliban for the right to lead a life of human dignity.

The world he sees in the over-dramatic light of an obsessed imagination.

No echoes of the old Faith stir in him. His children have the free directness of an unconquered race. No propitiatory rites are made either to the god of Methodism or of nature. His children shout across the fields, cursing by Christ and the Devil.

32

This is a world for the enchanted young, who learn at an early age that this rock-fragment which on a map is a drawing of a treasure island taking on an unreal fantasy in certain moods of summer weather, is set in an element too big for contemplation. The impact with reality is enough to unnerve a child.

Dai Penmon had hung a conger eel caught in the morning's fishing to dry for bait outside the boathouse after its throat and belly had been ripped open. In the afternoon Tudur saw it on his way down to the beach. The sun was burning its dead eyes and mouth. He ran a finger along the muscular body whose skin instantly contracted, wrinkling with a convulsive tremor, and the tail smacked out, striking him in the face. He ran screaming towards the men, away from the grinning conger eel. He stopped at the edge of the shingle and looked into the mysterious water which, it seemed to him, had suddenly become inhabited by serpents.

The child was told by his father that the eel would live though disembowelled and impaled, until sunset.

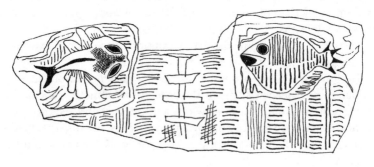

33

Siani was set to keeping the cattle from straying into the hay accompanied by a dog to snap at the cows' heels. The girl whistled and sang in a gruff boyish voice. Sitting motionless on a flower-covered bank she talked to her companions and listened to seals barking from the skerries. She had always been cut off from the companionship of other children; her parents never troubling themselves about whether she might be lonely or unhappy, so that she was tough even as a young child. By the time she was fourteen she had the self-assurance of a slum-dweller. She had worked out a system of complicated gymnastic feats on the rafters of the cowshed and she could be sly, bold, and fawning by turns; an unpleasant reflection of her parents' characters.

Sent to pick faggots on the mountainside, she would survey the extent of her world, from the lighthouse tall and shining to the ruined abbey and her father's farm. She seemed to see the world as an animal does. Her mind and heart never having been awakened, she showed no normal reaction to events; neither joy nor unhappiness nor awareness of pain, and was as unresponsive to the brutal ill-treatment meted out to her by her father as she was to the casual kindnesses of strangers. She had never learned to read or write or in fact to do anything but the roughest man's work; the result being that she was devoid of any femininity.

Siani listened to the sound of the sea, to the raging of the wind: rolling her eyes but saying nothing, while her mother kept up a mechanical chanting, 'Sticks! Sticks!' or, 'See to the cows!' But the child would be away, lured by the thought of wild green apples; slyly retreating to the corner of the mountain near the chapel where she could reach up for the sour green fruits.

34

Owain was fast asleep at the top of the bank, lying among weeds and flowers, on the edge of the potato field. His hoe lay along his arm, and his head was thrown back fully into the eye of the sun, its gold rays beating on the sleeping youth. There was barely any sound save from the sea and that was only a sleepy mutter of the tranquil waves. Answering the sun, a tide of yellow-blazing saffron flowers poured their gold in floods around him as he lay with open shirt and dusty pollen-coloured trousers; the sleeping shepherd under the noonday glare through the whole world's time.

Three suns stood over him, portentous in the west; the real light flanked by two pale mockers.

35

Nans returned from holiday, delighted for the space of a few hours, to be back on the island; disillusioned with the world represented by the nearest market town.

Wonderingly, she said, 'There isn't anything there' (as if she had expected magical visitations). 'What is there to see on the mainland to compensate for this?'

Her eyes drank in the fields, the cattle, and the sheep. It was the first time I had seen her happy. She had brought back much booty; boxes of fruit, and parcels; winter underwear filled the hand trunk.

In Cadwaladr's mailbag was a letter with a French postmark: a note from Paul in Paris, saying he thought he would be remaining there indefinitely. I pretended to myself that the news pleased me for his sake.

'The chances are ninety-nine to one that I shall be coming back,' he had said as we parted, as the train began to move away from the platform. He would come back in his own good time, no doubt.

After tea, we fished on a fairly strong swell right round the island, catching thirty mackerel and four pollack, in the huge switchback waves of the tideway; trailing our lines outside Maen Bugail and Craig y Llanw. When we were opposite my temporary furnitureless dwelling, Cadwaladr said to me as we slid up the back of a noble wave, 'There's your home.' We gutted the fish on the garden wall, with the rag-eared cat and the dogs, leggy pullets and hungry gulls, gathered round hoping for offal. A black-headed gull stood on the chimney-pot taking the last of the sunlight on his sinister wings. Cadwaladr glanced up from his work from time to time, to watch the surf creaming along the opposite coast.

The fish was split and salted and packed closely in an earthenware crock. The pot was carried into the dairy and covered so that flies could not get in. Fish keeps fresh this way even in the hottest weather.

36

Stewart had begun to take his furniture back the way it had so recently come. As the weather deteriorated towards winter, his and his wife's tempers worsened with it, until in a fit of final despair he had thrown in his hand and decided he could not go on fighting any longer against his wife's hatred of the island. Bits and pieces at a time, he transported chairs, beds, tables, and stored them in the boathouse on the other side of the water, where they soon mildewed or were gnawed by rats or were quietly spirited away. The Little Owl he gave to me as a parting gift. Doom settled himself firmly to live on the

frame of a picture, from which he could command the activities of
the kitchen. For long hours he would be silent, observantly stretching himself and opening wide his lovely golden eyes. His social life
began in the evening; when he would snap his beak, chitter, and
indulge in bad-owl language. When he became tired, he delighted
in being nursed, and would crouch down, hood his enormous eyes,
and quickly fall asleep.

37

It was as if a lion with spittle on his jaws prowled outside the door;
advancing first from the sou' west; then springing high; turning
about, to encounter a lion from the north. An unimaginable beast
from the north was in violent battle with the wild one from the
south west. The men braved the lion's claws to go over the Sound.
It was too rough to fish on the way across; too wild by the next tide
even to attempt the homeward crossing. The effect of the wind-
battle was fantastic. This was a test for beam and brace of any ship.

In the early part of the day, after the island boats had gone from us, no vessels passed; but in the afternoon, two coasters rising and falling in the grey troughs, came round into the shelter of the bay. The lions must have been harrying them as far as the headland.

A young female seal lay close inshore. She seemed reachable but she had made sure that a deep channel ran between her and possible danger. She was lying on her side stroking with a sensuous flipper her bulging hip. At times she scratched her head delicately; from time to time, stifled a yawn. She was fat, serious, and bloated with fish.

It was not until the next day that Cadwaladr and Owain in the *Cormorant*, and Stewart in the *Bridget Anne* were able to make a tentative start for the island.

Both boats had engine trouble, for water had got into their engines. Cadwaladr made for the shelter of the cove where he pulled up the boat, and fell to overhauling the engine. Stewart grimly remained on the sea, trying to get a spark of life from the magneto.

The father and son went for supper to one of the farms. When they returned to the cove, Stewart's deserted boat was on the shore and half-full of water. They had to wait until the ebb before they could pull it from the sea.

They had not finished with her until the early hours of the morning; and then it was Cadwaladr who took command of the situation. A hero then, in his true element, he swung his arms, flailed the air and shouted hoarse commands.

He ordered the open-mouthed Owain to bring all the dry kindling he could find into the boathouse. He made a fire and rough beds. The three men lay on damp sails until first light; Stewart wakeful and uneasy, already caught in a fever of sickness, Cadwaladr and Owain in a deep sleep. For the islandmen it was nothing new; they slept every night on the floor at home under bundles of old coats.

Just before noon they set out again, to make what was the worst crossing of Cadwaladr's experience up to that time. They were late starting on the tide and had to drive their engines hard against strong head winds. Before the boats made the island the wind was lifting the sea into boiling combers and gusty back-draughts rushed down the back of the mountain, carrying mists of spray through the Sound. They were favoured by one thing only; this wind being in the west, they had shelter once they were under the east cliffs.

38

There were plenty of mushrooms; so many indeed, that we found it difficult to make use of them all. I made mushroom soup every day and for breakfast we had them fried. On Sundays they were stuffed into green duck. They could have been sent to friends ashore if the weather had improved enough for the boat to go over. At last, I resorted to turning them into ketchup.

Mackerel were still about, and the deep gutters were full of rock-fish, that tasted better the colder the weather became. When the water was calm, they were plainly visible: bronze, lapis, green, orange, near the seabed passing from one jungle of weed to another. A conger eel writhed there too, in the clear depths. Weed bent forward through its branches before the wave-vibrations reached it; leaning in sinuous abandonment before the wave swilled over; then bending strongly backwards on the retreating water infinitely.

Cadwaladr and Dai, suddenly close friends in a courtesy father and son relationship, went fishing on the south end. Cadwaladr's rod was short and he fished a weedy spot. His gear was continually fouling until at last he broke the line and lost hook, line and sinker.

It was raining hard, the monotonous grey downpour of the west. Behind the rain pouring as if from a waterfall, I saw the relief ship passing through the Sound, and the red flash of the just-hoisted flag from the mast beside the lighthouse.

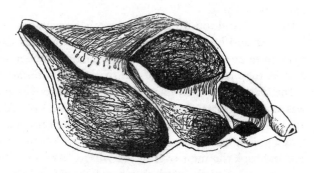

39

The islandmen in clear autumn weather were out from daybreak to dark, catching rabbits; intent on doing all the trapping they could while it was fine enough to get to market. The banks were full of gins; yellowing bracken concealed wire snares. Nights were horrible with screams of agony and deathly silences. The men went over to the coast at least twice a week, and were glad to be in bed early each night before the moon rose. The wind was not too favourable for the sea-passage, being mainly south east; a beam wind through the Sound made the seas choppy when there was only a moderate blow.

Now came overcast nights and wind off the land. Only a few weeks before, cabbage butterflies, hosts of fluttering wings, had passed over the summer sea. It would make a landsman's mouth water to be here in the early days of autumn for the feast of all sorts of birds: so many migrants dashed themselves to death on the tower of the lighthouse. After a thick night, the bodies of duck, curlew, snipe, woodcock, and other smaller birds lay broken on the ground.

Cadwaladr shot two seals, hoping to use their bodies for meat and oil. The first floated for a time but finally eluded him, being carried on the tide towards Pen Clogwyn, where he lost sight of it in the falling darkness. The other he shot in Bau y Pant, but it sank immediately; and though he watched out for it until the tenth day in case it should float to the surface, there was no sign of the body.

Cadwaladr went to fetch the new family moving into Clogwyn. They did not arrive in the village before dusk, so it was night before they put out to sea in a drizzly rain. It was Dic Longshanks and his wife Leah and four young children (so the infant population has gone up to nine).

He was forced to turn back by the roughness of the sea; the night was black and he had no compass. He tried the next day, but failed again to make the crossing. On the third day, the storm having abated a little, they were able to put out over a still turbulent sea.

The black bull which menaced our peace throughout the summer was silenced at last. Cadwaladr shot him instead of taking him over alive to the mainland, as he was afraid he might become enraged and kick a hole in the bottom of the old boat. He kept the offals for himself and took the meat over to the village. They were stranded there for eight days; on the ninth day they decided to take a chance. There was a strong swell breaking on the cove as they went along the high cliff path with sacks of groceries and coal. They returned to the beach at the village; managed to launch the boat, and crossed the bay to the cove where they loaded up. It was almost dark before they got away through a lashing storm of spray. Out of the influence of the ground-swell, their passage was easier.

Cadwaladr said: 'I look through peepholes, and I see facts.' And again: 'A man can make a living here, but it is a hard job very often. For anybody who likes a quiet and a peaceful life out of the world's turmoil, it is an ideal place.' And another time: 'When the chimney smoke goes straight up, we say the people are counting their money.'

40

Eira, the daughter of Rhiannon, Ty Draw, had a childhood memory of which she was never tired of telling me.

She had been crossing to the mainland in the island boat with her uncle and aunt of Clogwyn. She was seated on the knee of Dici Bach, a consumptive youth. Aunt Sarah, her mouth a doom-note, sat next to Eira's mother.

'Twm!' shrieked Sarah, packing into the cry the fear and spite she had hoarded since her last sea-excursion.

They were in the Sound when the engine slowed, rattled, and finally stopped. O there were waves, and rocks and whirlpools. Breakers lathered the cliff, black and wet and undeniable. The water hissed as it fell gravel-like into the boiling beer-foamed yards of slack. The lug-sail began to blow into shreds across the brows of the terrified children, and across Sarah's haggard face.

'Twm, why is it always calm when we start? Look at it now; it happens every time I go on the water with you,' she cried.

The men laughed as they pulled off their boots to use as bailing tins; they roared with reckless spirits as they sank them into the foam that swilled the scuppers.

'Twm, what good are you? O God, we shall sink. O God, why did I come with you only to be drowned?'

She wept huge hiccoughs over the child Eira, who, finding no comfort on the knee of the consumptive, had begun sobbing in

imitation of her aunt. The more the woman and girl cried, the more the men laughed. Twm grinned, wanting to be thought above the reach of his wife, yet forced to conciliate her. Cadwaladr, with both boots busy, his trousers rolled to the thighs, twitched his cap at a fresh angle and smirked, the grin beginning in his eyes. 'Dry your tears,' he said. He pinched Eira's arm.

Sarah began to pray: 'Dear God, forgive me for my sins. Forgive me for marrying a man like Twm, a no-good worthless man not fit to have charge of a boat. God, dear God, don't let me drown. I'll never go over the sea with him again, if only you'll let me live.'

Salt water gushed over her ankles. Bits of straw, bait, a sodden fragment of newspaper floated on its surface. A long-dead dogfish dried to a wrinkled knout of skin drifted back and fore in the filth. There was a smell of wood, salt, and corruption, and a hideous sound of untamed water. Gasps and moans of dismay escaped the women; the men cursed under their breaths. The boat lifted to a wave, and the bilge water ran away from the bows where Sarah sat, with the tears running down her neck. Feeling the water leave her shoes, she stopped a sob and said:

'It's better now.'

As the bow slid forward again over a green-smooth flood, she groaned, 'It's terrible, terrible. Why did I come? It will be the death of me.'

Eira remembered it as the day on which she had first known fear, learned it through the fear on her aunt's face.

It was many years since Dici Bach had died, Dici the consumptive boy who had gone over to the mainland with death on his back.

'He didn't die here,' she was careful to say.

'It is twenty years since anyone died here.'

41

I lost count of how many times Cadwaladr's new green engine failed that season. It had been yellow when new, but a sudden whim made him decide to repaint it green, the colour of ill-luck; so no one was surprised that he had so much trouble with it. He did most things by contraries, and I suppose that green was to him a lucky colour.

We were leaving the mainland beach; once again, the engine started, coughed twice, and stopped. Cadwaladr scraped the points with a knife and put the charred plug in a tin-full of ignited petrol to dry it off. We were sitting out in the bay; small flames licked the paint-work of the gunwale. The engine still refused to kick.

Cadwaladr sculled across to the cove, where Owain waited to carry me ashore.

No one was in sight when we landed; but by the end of an hour, I was one of a line of fishers. Twm's father appeared first, with a mountain pony and a rickety cart which he loaded with planks. The old man had a trilby hat pulled well down over his eyes to shield them from the strong sunlight. Composedly, he laid plank on plank until the cart was overladen; then with a loud cry and a flick of the reins, he urged the beast forward up the steep and narrow track, the pony almost invisible under the wood.

Fishermen drifted up until we sat in a row fronting the sea, waiting for the tide to turn. At one end sat a man famous for an experience in his far-away youth. He had a wen as big as a grapefruit on his neck.

He had been sent to screw down the coffin on an old woman who had died in the whitewashed cottage on the hill-top. When it was shut, he had to carry it along the path to the beach and then to the village. The box was on his back and he was at the steepest part of the way when the corpse began to squeak. The man gave one cry; dropped the coffin; and heeled it on to the sands. Now, he sat immobile in the evening light, his mind clear of the memory.

When one man turned to look at a circling bird, all turned. When one of us picked up a stone and threw it idly seawards, all threw stones. We were idle and contented so to be; until at the turn of the tide we bestirred ourselves; entered the boat once more and set out for a second attempt, Cadwaladr sculling close in under the land.

White horses waited at the entrance to the Sound. It was an Alpine landscape of spouting water; we were unprepared for rowing. While Cadwaladr swung his oar from side to side in skilful sculling, Owain hammered thole pins into the gunwales (and this was an echo of the long man with a wen on his neck, the man who had fastened the coffin of the old woman in the white cottage). Hammer-blows resounded from the cliff-sides. I looked at the two enormous oars that would have to take us to that elusive haven far out of sight. One of them was strong, the other had a broken-off blade.

Now as we came into the Sound, Cadwaladr, with a characteristic gesture, a movement deliberately overplayed, revealing the dangerous undercurrents of his nature by which he knows well how to affect the nerves of those around him, leapt amidships and took up an oar. It was more than his never-satisfied desire to overcome the sea, it was the desire to dominate his elder son.

'Row, you bastard, row.'

With trembling hands, his eyes terror-stricken, Owain set to work with the broken blade.

'In, out, in, out, rest your oar. Can't you see? Now, row for life. Don't take your eyes off the mark on the headland.'

Panting from his labours, Cadwaladr flung at me, as if his son had been no more than a dog:

'He's an idiot. He can't tell north from south.' Viciously, he shouted over his shoulder, 'Row east-by-south. Keep your eyes on the mark.'

It was as if Owain had been stricken dumb, deaf and blind. He simply rowed. Anywhere. Anywhere, so long as he could get away from his father. Breath whistled from his gaping mouth. The men rowed, strong as Vikings, between the swells; occasionally resting on their oars when a wave threatened to engulf the boat; trusting to the *Cormorant* to find her own way through the perilous half-hidden paths that can be followed by a cunning boat even in the most murderous seas. If ever a boat had native cunning, the *Cormorant* had it, with her heavy rolling gait, her out-thrusting snout over-riding the crests. Of all the island boats, she alone had this secret of the threading of waves, of passing between, never into the mountains of raving water. She carried us somehow in safety through deep valleys with nothing in sight but the toppling peaks overhead and endlessly breaking before us with the power of the wind behind the six knot race.

A yacht came in sight; she tacked, making heavy weather, off the black rock. Her sails trembling, she went warily round the black teeth of the islet; fighting for mastery over the unaccustomed waters of the Sound. The bright canvas shivered upright, pointed in our direction, flashing momentarily above the water peaks; isolated in the midst of hurrying foam, a yachtman in yellow oilskins moved on the gleaming deck; then the craft tacked again and fell away into the stormy darkness of the Irish Sea.

Raising my head from where I was bailing under a thwart, I saw Twm's boat sweeping in a flurry of foam towards the north end of the island.

It was like dropping through the seven seas, with tolling bells sinking round me.

Bending, I filled the tin dipper and emptied it overboard. Though the two men were putting out every ounce of strength we were being carried quickly out to sea. I could see the side of Maen Bugail whitened by surf. The roofs and chimneys of the farm went out of sight. Painfully, yard by yard, the boat was brought under the island out of the black whirlpools which had held the oars like an enchantment. At last, Owain could climb on to the bow and grapple with a boathook at a rock in the sheltered part of the cliff. I jumped ashore and made almost dizzy by the feel of the firm land after being in an open boat for six hours at a stretch without food, climbed stiffly but thankfully up the rocks to the hayfield; to the welcome smell of earth and grass and damp clover.

The farm was in darkness, except for firelight shining dully on the hearth. The table was set for supper, but there was no sign of Nans.

She was in the bottom fields, and she saw me above her in the dusk, and shouted brutally, 'Come down here.'

She was knee-deep in hay; her thin dress was dripping wet. She had mistaken me for one of the children in the half-light, not expecting me to arrive from the north end. I helped her to drive the cattle out of the hay; and then, after a cup of tea, I went down to the anchorage. The boat had just come in after a long struggle against the tide at the back of the seal cave. Cadwaladr was emptying letters out of the mailbag, and sorting them by candlelight in the boathouse.

Before crawling into the sleeping bag that night, I opened a parcel from home. There was a thick red jersey for fishing, a pair of shoes to replace my broken ones, and a letter from my mother asking when I was coming back to the mountains.

The next morning, when I awoke refreshed, vitality and happiness seemed to fill the sky. After such a bad crossing, with danger behind, it was like entering a new world of strength. Cadwaladr and Owain were making silage; Siani was there too, dripping with molasses. It was easy to laugh with them in the mild morning air about the trials of the previous night.

THREE

PAST SAINTS AND
PRESENT SINNERS

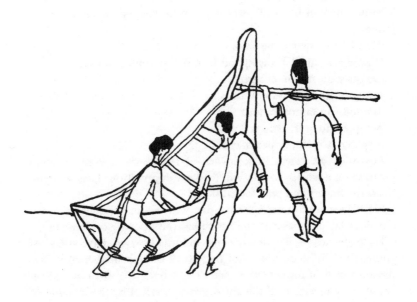

I

It is early January of the next year. It is night. In the lamp-lit kitchen I am ironing clothes for tomorrow's expedition which will be Paul's first, and my fourth visit to the island. Mounds of fragrant garments are airing in front of the fire. It has been the first clear day since Christmas; after more than three weeks of storm there is sunshine and a little wind.

Paul comes in from his room to say he has seen a spider in the corner.

'Good luck for us,' he says.

'A spider at night brings good fortune. In France, we say:
Araignée du matin, chagrin
Araignée du midi, ennui
Araignée du tantot, cadeau
Araignée du soir, espoir.
A spider at night, hope; may it be true.'

Anything, an insect in a corner of the room, a bird of good promise on a winter bough, will feed my superstitious heart tonight. Cross the fingers and pray for calm seas.

It has been an almost windless day with warm sunlight in which our dogs lay and basked. The house has the disorder of departure, a delayed departure. For nearly three months now we have talked of going, have lived in dreams of the island though neither of us has spoken much of his thoughts. Are we not both at a disadvantage? I, because my reverie is of the known rock overlaid by the weaving of imagination; and he? Since no one can understand the dreams of another when his own are of such tenuous structure, I cannot speak for him. This alone is certain: he has never been on the island, and so sees it through my eyes. How can we speak of anything that is to me tangible, a fragment of earth lived on by men and women who curse and laugh in gusts of spray; but is to him a place on a map, a thing of contours, a magnetic stone inhabited by unknown creatures. He feels the pull but cannot see the magnet. How can we speak of settling down there together when one of us has not yet visited the place?

We prepared ourselves for an open boat on a January sea; with windproof trousers, duffle coats, sheepskin gloves, and sea-boots.

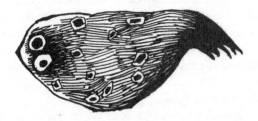

In a clear dawn the morning star stood white over the mountain. Thin wind, a fine swordblade out of the east, thrust a helm-cloud the length of the seven mile ridge of Carnedd Dafydd, to pour like milk into the dark valley.

How night cracks our mask of indifference! But how simple are our mornings; smoke rises, sorrow is pushed under the pillow; day mocks our night-spun passions.

In the glittering hours before winter noon, we pass from the fast-locked land of stone through scrubland and tree-bordered roads almost to the tip of the peninsula.

How different an air our port of embarkation wears in wintertime, with no one but ourselves moving in the street. The two hotels and the boarding house are shut, and hanging askew on the door of the small café is a black card with white letters spelling SHUT framed in ice and many-pointed stars of frost.

Only the sea is abroad; along the desolate beach run hungry waves that would like to devour the houses and the hotel; the grave-yard and the church at the top of the strand.

Waves do at times flood in fury through the village so that the sea-god's emblems are flung about the pathway; whorled horn of whelk, brittle-sheathed razor-shell; garland and shining mound of weed. Here it is as if there was on earth no voice so powerful as that of ocean.

At dawn, fisherfolk stood at their windows on which ran salt sprays. Under the hump-backed bridge, lay the river dumb with ice and snow. A face at a window was watching another grey face in the house opposite. Each face was printed with the awareness of the sea. Surf and shingle thundered, as if to destroy the stones of the few houses. A green swell engulfed the twin transepts of the church. The doors were silted up with sand, and bladder wrack hung in bunches from the inn-signs. Shells and glass lobster-floats the colour of deep water, lay in snow drifts. Sandgrains and snowflakes mingled. And then, when the tide slowly withdrew down the sea valleys, there was left in the middle of the road one petrified wave crusted with salt and a skin of ice, rearing ready to fall, the spray from its crest congealed into icicles.

This was the winter death.

We were doubtful whether a boat could put in through such a swell. Without pausing for food, we started up the hill towards the sacred well, for the purpose of signalling by fire to the island. There was an icy wind out of a clear blue sky. It was the first day of the great frost of 1947. Hedgers greeted us, crying out that it was enough to freeze the blood; but we, under packs, and with the speed of our walking, could scarcely breathe for heat. One mile, two miles, two and three-quarter miles we followed the telegraph poles up and down-hill until we arrived at the end of the peninsula. Beyond swelling ground and lost in haze was a smoke-blue mountain.

'What is that other headland?' asked Paul.

'It is the island.'

Passing through a gate, we went down frozen grass-slopes to the well of purification. So, in that calm afternoon of frost before the blizzard struck the whole countryside, Paul came with me to the pool in the rocks where on that headstrong Sunday afternoon in the previous summer, I had prayed for his return. There was no echo in me now of that summer day. The link was only made complete in memory. At that moment there was only the distant sea-rock lying in the smoke and dust of the afternoon; and around it the surf.

What is that murmur in the wave-scoured cavern-foot, with a bird-call crying: Come back?

He has returned; he is beside me. Together, we stare at the black cone tilted to the sun. He is wearing his scarlet pirate's cap.

For this crossing, we had had careful instructions from Cadwaladr. In the first letter he had said:

'Signal by fire from above the well, as near as possible to the bottom of the gorse patch. We will answer from the field near the mountain. As soon as you see our smoke put out your fire, and we will quench ours, so that we shall both understand that it is a signal for a boat and not someone making a gorse fire for pleasure or clearance of the land (that's the reason you are to make the fire at the bottom of the bracken above the well) and don't forget to put out your fire when we light one here; so don't fire a patch that is likely to spread too much, but try to find a small clump of gorse. If we think the sea is too rough or any crisis on the farm should stop us from coming; we will relight our fire a minute or two afterwards. In this way, you would not have to wait indefinitely.'

We lit a fire that on the tongue of flame leapt backward down the centuries. The gorse cracked; flame and smoke poured away on the wind over the cold and choppy sea, while the cavern under the well boomed with surf.

The sun stood in the west; our slope was strongly lit; the island was in haze. I tried to concentrate on the field at the mountain foot, for I knew that the answering signal would be lit there. Whenever I looked away to rest my eyes, orange stains blotted the sky.

After about an hour a plume of smoke rose from the island. It seemed miraculous that a flame should have been struck from the sombre rock. Overjoyed, we leaped up and stamped out our fires, until our boots grew hot.

They had only lit one beacon on the island. Good; it meant they were coming for us; and that in about an hour they would be in the Sound. We huddled against the piercing cold in a rock bay; after a time, I thought I heard the throb of an engine far away, but it came no nearer. There was no sign of any craft.

Another, much bigger beacon burned up in the farm field over there. At last it looked as though they were coming for us. To show that we were still at the well, and to warm ourselves, we made a fire at which we crouched eagerly.

The sun was sinking; the earth becoming colder and colder. The red and misshapen sun fell from the sky.

We sat over the flames, squatting now by this, now by that bed of glowing ash, while the ground became ever more intensely frozen. At last we lost heart, and grew weary of watching the grey emptiness of the Sound.

Suddenly, another beacon went up from the island. Once more we put out our fires and waited for the second signal from Cadwaladr.

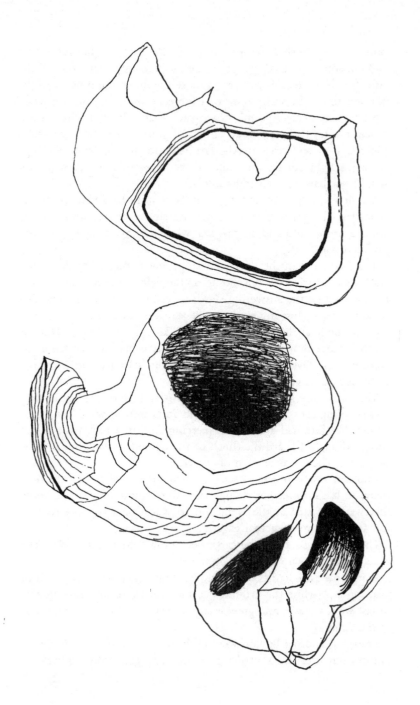

In a few minutes it came. Further along the island field there was a red glow, then smoke poured towards the west. So they could not come for us; there must be engine trouble or a cow was calving, or it was too late on the tide. Dispirited and hungry, we trudged back to the village through the dusk.

The next morning, we were out early on the beach, watching the headland for a boat; and to cool our impatience, walked to the far end of the shore. The sea was empty. An old woman in black wandered for a while at the edge of the tide. In the village they said that no one would set out in such weather from the island, with the wind blowing so strongly from the north west.

Only Cadwaladr might do it. 'He's the only man who might,' said one. 'He's willing to take a risk.'

After lunch, carrying with us only a few things, we went again to the well. As on the previous day, we lit a fire in the grass. Five minutes later, smoke rose from the farm field. Yesterday, I had wasted too much emotion; today, I was determined to show no interest until the boat was actually in view. So I lay down, washed of all feeling.

Paul had walked over the brow of the headland. After an hour he came back shouting loudly.

'The boat! The boat!'

He was trembling violently, and his arm shook as he pointed towards the Sound. It was only then I realised how much the journey meant to him, and it left me dumb with surprise. A black speck was moving in shadow of the island, rising and falling in the troughs.

At last we could make out that it was an old man and a youth in her; and we went to meet them, climbing down a wet gully to the surf-washed islet. The boat was close in, the engine cut off. Cadwaladr was standing, one arm at the tiller, the other signalling as an aid to his voice, which was scarcely audible above the crash of water. We leaped across a channel through which the surf creamed, thinking the boat could approach close enough for us to jump aboard.

A muffled shout came from the man.

'Not there! We cannot come near enough to you. The boat would be smashed. Come over here, to the other side.'

We leapt back over the lathering water. Paul started to climb across the naked rock, but half-way up he was arrested by the voice of Cadwaladr.

'Not there; that place is no good, either. You must cross to the other side of the mountain. We will go to meet you at Porth Felen.'

As we climbed the steep hill-side, we caught glimpses of the boat racing round the headland of Trwyn y Gwyddel. We scrambled over miniature escarpments until we came to a gully leading to the inlet. We slid on wet clay and turf; here, the swell was less felt. A small promontory completely covered with seaweed ran out into the sea. It was necessary to sit astride the slippery rocks and to slide cautiously forward. Paul took a standing jump into the boat. Cadwaladr's face was anxious.

'Be quick,' he commanded me. 'Or we'll be on the rocks.'

We slid forward. The boat was rolling heavily to the swell. When we were both aboard we sat, dishevelled and dirty, panting still from our race over the headland. Cadwaladr and Owain were grinning. The father gave his cap a twist and thrust out his hand.

'How are you?'

We shook hands, laughing at a show of manners in such a situation. Owain gave his father the handle of the engine. The engine remained dead. Owain took out the plug and cleaned it. When he put it back, the engine gave not so much as a cough.

'I shall have to cool her down a bit,' said Cadwaladr. 'She's hot because we had to race her against the tide in the Sound.'

We drifted in towards the rocks. Cadwaladr sculled, his eyes sharp and ready for danger. He swung the handle again. The engine throbbed, the boat went forward, the cliffs slid away; we were in the Sound, moving towards the shadowy island.

Paul and I sat together in the bows. He turned to me triumphantly.

'At last,' he said. 'We are nearer to the island than I have ever been before.'

'Don't say that; never speak about the island until you are across the Sound.'

I think it seemed to him that we were a long time between shore and shore, for he said at intervals:

'Is it much further? How far is it to the anchorage?'

We tracked through water lanes, this way, that way. The sea was what Cadwaladr calls neither good nor bad. Swells ran under the boat, and we would find ourselves flung sideways as a wave piled itself against our frail craft. The water was at its roughest along the back of the island mountain where wind and tide combined against us. We had to sit in the stern so that the bows should be free to ride lightly on the hurrying waves; even with the engine at full speed we remained stationary opposite a deep gully for a long time. The propeller threshed the water, but we scarcely moved.

At last, we ran out of the strongest pull of the current at Pen Clogwyn, and knew that we should soon make landfall.

2

At Pant, in the room facing south-east, I was put to sleep in a room with the elder daughter, Myfanwy. The storm kept me awake for most of the night. Paul slept on the old clothes chest downstairs in the kitchen; and at times during the night, I heard him swearing under his breath, and throwing things at the mice which kept up a persistent busyness in the weighing scales, in the table drawer, and among the piles of old newspaper in a corner.

Siani came in to stand at the bedroom window while it was still gloomy and sad before dawn. It was almost impossible for her to see through the frosted panes. She rubbed clear a tiny peep-hole, and I glimpsed beyond her shoulder, sheep huddled together on the frozen earth. It was a relief to get up, to put on jerseys and wind-proof clothing after the cold shivering of the night, during which Myfanwy and I had lain close together for warmth.

A day of unbroken frost and thick fog succeeded this bitter night.

At the Cafn, the men discussed whether it would be safe for the boats to cross to the mainland. Cadwaladr ran along the shore like a wild man pursued by devils; only to report that the swell was impossibly savage.

The lighthouse relief ship was expected in the afternoon but failed to come.

Paul and I walked the west coast beside a roaring surf of glass and cream. The waves were empty of seals; gulls were sitting about on the land above the sea, waiting patiently for the storm to blow itself out.

It was still too soon, I dared not ask Paul what he thought of living here. There were long silences between us.

At night, among bundles of willow wands, tarry junk, the smell of engine oil, we talked with Cadwaladr in his workshop, Hen Dŷ. He had a habit of shutting himself in there with thoughts and projects that never bore fruit; while his sons, in a cowed silence split willow wands for the new season's lobster pots.

Later, in the kitchen, with warm firelight shining on the slate hearth, I read (unnoticed by the card-players at the scrubbed table) the legend of Dyfrig Beneurog in an old book of Cadwaladr's.

Dyfrig had a tall and beautiful mother, a proud princess flattered by mirrors and suitors who told her she was rare as a birch tree in a forest of oaks. She had this one son, a love child lapped round with the customary tall marvels even before his birth. One day, her father the king went out hunting the wild boar where they rooted hopefully among the primeval acorns. Returning from the chase, he shouted loudly for his daughter.

'Daughter,' he said, 'daughter, will you wash my hair? There wasn't a breath of wind in the forest, our horses threw up clouds of dirt; we were bitten all over by midges. My head itches; so, daughter, wash my hair.'

She brought silver vessels; a ewer, towels, cold and hot water. The king bent his head, and she began the washing. Now, the king happened to look out of his streaming hair, and the middle of her was in his line of vision. Her belly was like a wine-cask, greatly swollen with child. He leapt up, overturning the water basin, and he pushed the wet tails of hair from his eyes. He shouted, 'Drown her; drown her.'

Servants dragged her away to the sea; her father believed her drowned; but the ninth wave tossed her back dry and unhurt on to the beach.

The king raged, seeing the girl rise up. He sent for dry kindling, for branches of the forest trees, and ordered a fire to be lit round her body. The flames seemed to consume her, but when the fire had died down, they found her sitting in the warm ashes with a child in her lap.

The king gave up fighting against fate; accepted the child, and sent him to the best schools. Eventually, he mastered both human and divine laws, and became known as a holy man.

A band of devout fishermen, wishing to erect an oratory to safe-guard themselves against dangers at sea, went to him in this matter.

Not caring to be rushed, he said, 'Let me think a little. I'll take a walk, and pray for a sign.'

He wandered aimlessly about among the pebbles and weeds of the shore, and met with a sow and nine piglets wallowing in a muddy pool.

'A good omen,' muttered the saint. Carefully, he herded the swine into a high and advantageous place overlooking the sea where he decided (with the pig-aided guidance of divine providence) the oratory should be built.

Years went by, until Dyfrig in his old age was made a bishop. Then, one day he suddenly threw up the honours of the church; the rock-hump in the Sound was calling him. And there he joined the community of saints, and lived with sea-fowl until he died in the year of our Lord, 612.

In the days before lighthouse and submarine he lived there (near where I am now sitting) among the puffins and the guillemots. And he said:

'I bless these birds that breed here in the spring of the year: and I give them a double-luck blessing when they fly away towards their winter homes. I bless the henbane dark under the influence of Saturn. I bless the pure water gushing from the stone. I bless sun, moon and stars. My God, I raise above these things, for he turns the moon on his hand; the stars are trapped in his hair.'

Few men are saints, but all saints are human beings. What of Dyfrig's carnal life? It was not only Jacob who wrestled with an angel. At night in his young manhood how he must have raved; needing a woman, then filled with remorse.

You dreamed of a woman's thigh imprinted with the shape of fronds from your bed of fern; and fled into the light of safe morning. At the water's edge, you lay for a long time in the rain. God neither struck nor solaced you, poor old man. And why should he? You were left in a vacuum kneeling there, beside a stranded jelly-fish.

What is your celibacy now? If you had left one human phrase for us, 'The sun dancing on water sets up a shimmering reflection; transparent shapes dazzle on the roof of my cave,' or words such as these: 'Today, a woman came from the mainland with a gift of fresh-baked bread. She was beautiful in charity,' we could have loved you, finding the living rose in the dry chronicles.

Who has filled up with earth the mouth of the anchorite's cell, where the once golden-headed man lies dead?

They are still playing cards, the ardent boys; laughing loudly. Tudur is flushed with victory. At the hearth sit the parents with bowed backs and dull eyes. There is nothing left between them, no ground for companionship. He has his love-affair with the sea; but the woman, withdrawing each year more stubbornly into herself, has become soured by obscure resentments and the bitter cancer of jealousy.

Cadwaladr shut his eyes, crouching further over, to hide himself from his wife's scrutiny.

'Cadwaladr,' said she.

'What do you want?'

'Cadwaladr, where will you bury me when I'm dead?'

'Under the cairn on top of the mountain; with a ginger beer bottle beside you if you like, with your name in it.' It was quiet in the kitchen. There was a smell of old people sitting among rags and misery.

'Nans,' said Calwaladr.

'What?' said she.

'Where do you want to be buried?'

'In the churchyard of the village over the water; as any respectable woman would want to be.'

From the look he gave her, he might have been thinking, 'Once dead, you'd do as lobster bait.'

There is a saying among the mainlanders:

'The people of the island would use anything for bait; children, or their own mothers.'

Listening to them, I began to feel my way towards the poem that was to be called 'Islanders'.

> Full of years and seasoned like a salt timber
> The island fisherman has come to terms with death;
> His crabbed fingers are coldly afire with phosphorus
> From the night-sea he fishes for bright-armoured herring.

Lifting his lobster pots at sunrise,
He is not surprised when drowned sailors
Wearing ropes of pearl round green throats
Nod their heads at him from underwater forests.

His black-browed wife who sits at home
Before the red hearth, does not guess
That only a fishscale breastplate protects him
When he sets out across ranges of winter sea.

3

The grandfather clock is an enemy telling me that death runs at my heels. The clock has a painted face picturing the four seasons: Spring, a child on a sheep-covered hill; Summer, a girl big with child raking hay in a shining meadow; Autumn, a woman blown before a tempest; Winter, an old man with a red face pushing sticks into a fire under a cooking pot slung from a tripod. There is a painted moon behind, that moves with the days of the month.

4

A thin line of smoke trailed from the horizon; it was the relief ship at last. The flag went up at the lighthouse, and we hurried to the anchorage in time to see the tender bringing in the first load of coal and oil. The seamen were rolling ashore the oil drums thrown overboard into shallow water. One man in a woollen cap stood thigh-deep, drawing the drums along with a boat-hook towards the waiting carts. The old horse was twenty years old and pulled from custom with his aged muscles the cart containing two fifty-gallon drums of oil. The other horse, a chestnut three-year-old was only allowed to pull the weight of one drum. He took the steep shingle with a rush, his eager muscles quivering under the smooth skin.

Leaving the scene of activity, I went into the storehouse to find Paul standing at the dusty window, watching with a melancholy expression the movement on the beach below.

There was a bitter grey light, and a dangerous gleam on the waves to the sou' west that put me in mind of long knives and fish eyes. The action was framed by the weed-covered rocks on either side of the beach: off-shore, the tender wallowed in a heavy swell.

5

Dai Penmon's light was shining in the front upstairs room. Myfanwy, Siani and I went up the dark staircase to the bedroom where he had made up a good fire of coals.

Bundles of fresh-cut withies lay on the floor; in the corner were his newly-made lobster pots. We sat about on coils of rope and boxes, stretching out our half-frozen fingers to the flames.

Children had scored their names deep into the plaster of the walls. 'Myfanwy loves Dai. Dai loves Alice. Dic is a fool.'

Dai paused in his work to look at the fire. He said:

'This is always better than over there,' meaning the mainland.

Myfanwy retorted at once, 'I'd rather be on the mainland; it's like being a prisoner, living here. And yet, I want to stay here, too . . . '

With a play of eyes, she is constantly trying to rouse Dai, who remains indifferent to her. She is bent on some secret life of her own; she is young, reaching out to womanhood, quite lost in the stirring of blood. Pushed round the house at the tail of her mother's grumbling; peeling potatoes, washing floors, cleaning the grate, she is intent on the moment of release when she can merge her newly awakened sexual feelings with the fortunes of a novelette heroine, or run out to Dai where he works at his baskets.

Nans gave us brywes for supper. To make this, she crushed home-made oatcakes; to which were added bread, buttermilk, pepper and salt, fat and boiling water. The bowls of brywes were left covered for a time on the hob by the fire.

Of what is Paul thinking as he laughs over the playing-cards?

We bowed to the new moon in the west; then Paul carried Siani high on his shoulders. She, delighted, wanted him to slide on the ice with her on his back.

The young wife of Dic Longshanks followed by three of her children met us on the path. She was weighed down by buckets of water.

A dark figure came lumbering towards us: it was Cadwaladr, with whom we went down to the storehouse where we picked up our provisions. We walked home in procession, each carrying a heavy load. On the way up, Owain told us, his voice happy as if with good news, of the mishap that had prevented their return the night before.

'There was a heavy ground-swell,' said the simpleton. 'After launching the boat, we got aboard her and thought to make the quieter water safely. I braced the boat-hook in the sand, but it got stuck; so I lost hold of it, and my father began to row. A great wave came up, driving the boat on to the boat-hook and breaking it. The boat got out of control, and lay broadside on to the waves. The swell broke over, half swamping her. We had to leap overboard up to our waists in the sea and throw out all the gear. It was an hour before we recovered everything and had emptied the boat of water and sand. We had lodging for the night on one of the farms, but before they would give us supper, even before we were allowed to change our clothes, we had to move bales of straw in a barn so that we could have a place to sleep.'

6

'There was my boy,' said the King to me one day.

'Two nights after he went deep-sea fishing, we had the sign. We heard the rattling of bones; and that was the way we knew he was drowned and crying out for burial; or if not already dead, must be in terrible danger and in need of our prayers. After the bone-rattling, there was a silence for a few days, and then he suddenly turned up on the beach. True enough, it was our son; we knew him by the silver dollar at his throat; but no stranger would have known him. He was dumb and heavy as clay, and his eyes were blind for ever.

His mother became strong when she saw him, though he was a salty corpse; for now she had him safe at home, and after a short time she could smile when she pointed out his grave whose mound she had covered with sea-flowers. You understand, it comforts a woman to be able to say, he lies safe in the earth. To have him always near her, though silent, gave her a measure of courage. The madness went out of her eyes; they were no longer red-rimmed and staring, stung with spray from looking past the living to the empty waves.'

He lost himself in a far-off dream, and said:

'The islands of the dead . . . When we were children, we used to play on the shore of the bigger of those two islands; cooking our morning porridge under a dry-stone wall on a fire of bleached birch-twigs. Sometimes, a black-throated diver would be fishing on the fresh morning water.'

I looked at the beer-pickled, briny scoundrel, and asked:

'Are you afraid of evil spirits?'

He laughed, and assumed an embarrassed seriousness.

'Some men think there's a devil that destroys lobster pots and over-turns fishing boats; and they do say that if a boat has had the evil eye put on it, she will never be trustworthy until she has been blessed by a priest with holy water.'

Sensing that he had my full interest, and that I was not likely to laugh at him, he went on:

'This is the truth I'm telling you, about these same islands of the dead. A man I knew went over there once with his lady-love. It was a windy day; he stepped aside to light his pipe behind a bush, and when he turned round the girl had vanished utterly.'

7

In his irreverent old age, the King was scarcely known to work; he walked but rarely, being content to sit in contemplation of his

kingdom; when he did move, it was only to go slowly to the Cafn
if there was a good chance of a yacht putting in to the island, for
visitors were always impressed by his crown, his beard, and his
royal thirst.

The pockets of his coat gaped wide from the carrying of many beer
bottles. Meeting a visitor, he would growl:

' . . . throat's like the bottom of a parrot's cage.' And it was the
sound of thunder trapped on a mountain ridge.

After the death of his wife, all manner of women had wooed him
unsuccessfully, thinking to become queens, though the kingdom
might be only a few yards of turf and stone. A countess from the
Bavarian alps had written to him in a perfumed hand, proposing
marriage; but he had laughed hugely, and put away the letter in an
old stained chest with the rest of his correspondence.

He was still possessed of great physical strength, which he needed
in his position as sovereign and policeman and prime minister.

Once, when he was fishing (in his seventieth year) a giant skate
became attached to the side of his boat by suction; the King leaned
over the gunwale, placed his hands round the sides of the fish and
bit into the beak; then wrenched it inboard so violently that it
almost landed in the sea at the other side of the boat.

8

The King having been a widower for many years, lived with his
kinswoman Sarah and her love-child, her husband Twm and their
son Samson, in one of the double-houses, Clogwyn. He detested
Dai, and treated him as an outcast. They had lived together for
many years before Sarah had married Twm.

In the evenings of the past, the old man had been in the habit of
sitting so close to the fire that the boy and his mother had had no
warmth from it.

'If you feel cold,' the old man would shout, 'go over to the west
side and gather driftwood for your own fire. This hearth is mine!'

One morning the woman had got ready to go out into the fields to milk the cows. Before she went, she gave a Welsh cake and a clean pocket handkerchief to her child.

When they were alone together, the King said:

'I want you to go to my sister who lives in the sea off the west side. Tell her I sent you, and ask her for some strong twine to mend my herring nets.'

The little boy put on his best striped shirt, and set out, taking with him the cake and the handkerchief.

He said to himself, 'I will pass the time of day with Jacob. He will advise me what I should do.'

Jacob was scything a field of hay in the south of the island.

'How do?' he shouted. 'Where are you off to, my lad?'

'Uncle Jacob,' said the boy, 'my foster-grandfather has sent me to visit his sea-sister, to ask her for strong twine to mend his nets. I thought I had better come to you first for advice.'

'What a good thing,' exclaimed Jacob. 'How cunning you are. Your foster-grandfather's sister is nothing but an old bitch. Now, listen to me. In her so-called palace, but which is really a smelly cave, stands a looking-glass which she talks to as she tries out her magic. She is sure to ask you to polish it; that sort of woman always tries out that sort of trick. Be careful to use the clean hand-kerchief your mother gave you this morning. And don't scratch the surface of the glass, whatever you do. If you talk to it respectfully, it may tell you what to do if the queen casts a spell over you. It may even happen that the queen will try to make you lose your memory.

You know the little painting of your father which your mother keeps in a drawer at home? Remember it well. If by chance, you should see it again whilst under an enchantment, your memory will come back. Keep a lion's heart, and you will get the better of the king and his sister.'

'Good-bye, and thank you,' said the child.

'Good-bye, and bless you,' said the man.

The boy comes to the strand; shuts his eyes, and dives under the waves.

At last he reached the sea-queen's cave. She was seated in front of her mirror.

'Good morning,' said the boy.

'Good morning to you,' said the queen. 'And what can I do for you?'

'Foster-grandfather, your brother, sent me to ask for a ball of twine to mend his fishing nets.'

'Very well. I will go and fetch twine so strong that no fish can tear it. While you are waiting, sit down in front of the mirror. Be a good boy, and polish it for me.'

The boy set to work, using the soft handkerchief his mother had given him. Following his uncle's advice, he began talking to the glass.

'Kind looking-glass, what will she do to me?' The child continued with his work, rubbing gently, until the stripes of his shirt shone as brightly in the mirror as they did on his breast.

He heard the queen laughing behind him. She called out to one of her servants. 'Such a fine pretty boy has come to see me this morning. When he has finished polishing the mirror, I will change him into a seal.'

The servant came into the room. She muttered to herself.

'How sad his mother will be, to lose him.'

The child tried to feel brave; so, turning to the servant, he asked, 'What do you think of my polishing?'

'You have worked well, but do not hurry yourself.'

'Why not?' asked the child.

At first, the servant pretended not to hear; then, coming close to him, she whispered:

'The mirror knows more than I do.'

The child begged, 'Please, help me to escape.' Again she pretended not to hear. The boy felt in his pocket for something with which to bribe her. His fingers closed on the little cake.

'Here,' he said, 'is a cake from the world that is lit by the sun.'

The servant, who had never before tasted anything like it, thought the cake was wonderful. She ate half of it, and wrapped the rest in her handkerchief. Coming up close to the boy, she whispered, 'I cannot prevent her from turning you into a seal if she wants to; but I know of one spell that will perhaps have the power of making you human again. A loving woman must comb your body.'

'It is evening in the world,' thought the child. 'Mother will have laid supper on a white cloth. There will be fresh milk and ryebread, and butter stamped with the shape of a swan.'

'Is the mirror clear, is the mirror fair?' called out the queen.

'The mirror is clear as a lake,' answered the child. The woman touched the child lightly with the first finger of her left hand, saying:

'Be neither fish nor flesh nor mortal from this time on. Go! But before you go, look at yourself.'

Was it his, that round, whiskered head, that thick furry body?

The doors of the cavern flew open, and the young seal shuffled out through the dark halls until he found himself in the open sea. He swam as fast as light to the surface of the water, which gleamed with phosphorescence under the moon. As he rose to breathe in air, the moon's calm radiance shone into his eyes, drawing him up. Sinking again, he twisted and turned, pleased with his new power. A fleet of silver-green fishes passed far below him. Plunging, he snapped at the leading fish.

After he had satisfied his hunger with herring and rock-fish, he began to feel lonely. Stretching his neck out of the sea, he gazed round to see in the westward, a small island. Though he did not recognise it, over there was his home.

He began swimming towards the island, sometimes keeping to the gloomy depths, sometimes among the moonlit waves. At length, he reached the broken rocky shore. He dragged himself up to rest on a flat stone covered with red weed.

In the morning, as soon as it began to grow light, the lad's mother came down to the strand, for she had spent a night of despair. When she had come home from the fields the evening before, she had asked the King:

'Where is the boy?'

'I don't know. This morning, he went out to pick sticks, and he has not come back.'

The mother came to where the seal lay.

'Since by this time, my boy must be dead, I will adopt this baby seal,' she said to herself. Creeping up, she clasped him firmly in her arms. The seal cried out and moaned like a human child but the woman did not let go, even when he bit and scratched her. She carried the creature home, and put him in her son's old cradle.

The King laughed when he saw what she had brought home.

'Aha,' he said. 'My fine fellow; you will be tasty to eat; your fat will do to grease my boots; and what a warm jacket your skin will make.'

To comfort herself a little, the woman took out of the drawer in the kitchen dresser, the picture of her dead lover. The cradle was standing in the window, and as the woman moved to let the light fall on the painting, the seal was able to see what it was she was holding. When he saw the portrait, his memory came back.

He cried out in a shrill voice, 'Mother, mother; comb my fur.'

The woman was almost frightened out of her senses. At last she found a comb and began to smooth his dappled coat. The fur began to fall off. Soon, what had been a seal, was again the widow's son. Weeping for joy, the mother embraced him.

'Come with me, my child,' said the mother. 'We must tell the news.'

After the story had been told to the other islanders, the men of each household armed themselves with stout poles, and every woman filled her apron with stones, and the children took up their catapults. In a body, they went down to the anchorage where the King sat peacefully chewing tobacco. They drove him before them into the water, and he had to swim out to escape the sticks and stones. Now that his cruelty had been discovered, he knew the islanders would not have him back again. So he decided to go and live with his sister on the mainland. He swam until he was within hailing distance of a lobster boat from the village; and went away, with never a glance behind at his lost realm.

9

A grey strand sucked and pounded by the ocean: and above the highest-lying belt of wrack, the stone house with its roots in shingle.

In a black storm before cock-crow, the sea loosed itself at the coast, with dreadful suddenness, while the men were fishing far out, steepling the rollers' backs, and gliding with tight hearts into green troughs boiling to the horizon.

On the roof of the house, braving the sting of salt and sand sprayed up from the bursting seas, sat Siani and Tudur. Solemn as little owls or ghostlike sorcerers under a blear-eyed moon, they gripped the ridge-tree; with wide-stretched legs they struggled to keep in place the rattling slates. They gleamed with a blue radiance from sheets of spume; they were luminous wraiths in the midst of night.

Nans moaned into the folds of her shawl. She cried out suddenly to her children.

'Stop looking . . . that old green grave.'

Turning to Rhiannon, she said bitterly:

'That whore out there wants all our men and won't be content till she gets them.'

She fell silent, wondering how many of the men were drowned. Had their boats foundered, or were they riding the sea stripped of

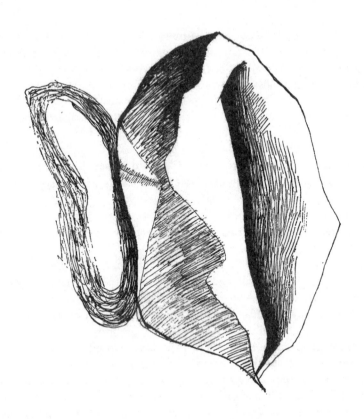

sail and gear, to be cast up on the rocks a half-year hence?

Myfanwy, whose lover, Dai Penmon, was one of those out at sea, gazed bleakly, prematurely aged, towards the green underworld. She seemed to be walking there in her heart with bones for company, in the kingdom where skeletons grow rich with purple-frilled anemones and the gold-armoured barnacle; skeletons whose skulls' eye-pits are inhabited by hermit-crabs, and whose limbs are clutched by hermit crabs. She seemed to be watching the wild erotic dances of nereids and syllids. In her intense frowning absorption, she might have been witnessing the cycles of the sea.

She bent down to pick up a shell; and sniffed it to catch the faint tang of salt; holding it to her ear, she heard a blurred hissing and rumbling of surf.

Myfanwy is no longer the simple, compliant girl of last year; there is a great strife in her, the elemental fighting of new loyalties against old: the call of awakened blood, duties, inhibitions, a longing for happiness, and the strong pulling of the dead.

10

Cadwaladr was repairing a net in the old house. The island lofts were full of new lobster pots and nets. The pots were of two kinds, French and Welsh.

The old man said:

'Yesterday, three herring nets were washed up from a wrecked trawler on the beach at Hell's Mouth.'

In the afternoon, Paul and I went to the south end, where we sat under a sheltering wall and spoke of plans to live here. At last I dared to ask him whether he would care to farm and fish here. Had he shown any hesitation, I should have known that everything was over.

He said, 'Of course, of course. I think it is wonderful.'

Frozen snow on the window; a gale howling out of the north. Contentment began to grow in me. By a smoky wood fire in the old house, we sat and peeled hazel wands as fast as Cadwaladr could split them. Tudur, Owain, Cadwaladr, Paul and I were happily and silently at work. The whittling knives shone, the skinned wands fell to the floor, the muscles played in Cadwaladr's arms as he eased the blade down the centre of the wood. When we paused to throw more kindling on the fire or to rest our tired backs, we talked of the French crayfishers whose pots were the inspiration for those now fashionable with the islandmen. Bretons first fished these waters about thirty years ago, a short time before the old islanders left. The Bretons were last here during the Second World War, in the sultry days of the fall of France. At that time, they were on their way back to Brest, anxious to find out what had happened at home.

The French crabbers were in the habit of fishing within the three mile limit for crayfish which bring good prices in France, compared with the prices in this country, where lobsters are considered the greater delicacy.

The Breton boats had lain at anchor, and the men had been invited ashore with fair words. Ovens were lit, hens' necks were wrung, pastry was rolled out on cool slate slabs.

'Come inside. Make yourselves at home; there is plenty to eat.'

The women and old men smiled and gestured to make themselves understood. Meanwhile, the young men were busy on the sea, stealing the French pots. They hid them about the island; and on the next day, when the Frenchmen had discovered the treachery, they were approached in a different mood. The women went out to meet them as decoys and blinds, whilst the men remained at home to guard the pots. Wherever they went, the foreigners were met with bland smiles and mock courtesy from the women. They fared no better with the men, and were forced to go back to their boats, unsatisfied.

After the Bretons had gone, the Welshmen made a close study of the stolen pots. Unlike the round Welsh type, these were cylindrical in shape. The trap openings were larger, since the baskets were originally intended for catching crayfish. It was necessary to go round the pots more frequently with this type, since it was comparatively easy for the shellfish to escape. Many of the glass floats now used by the islandmen to mark their pots were part of the gear stolen from the Breton poachers.

'There was a running fight once,' says Cadwaladr, 'between an island boat and a French vessel. There was a bit of an argument between them while they were fishing, and the Frenchmen gave chase. They threw curses like hailstones at each other, revelling in the juice of language. It came to violence at last; the French hurling planks at the smaller Welsh boat in hopes to damage her. It ended in a dogfight, with neither getting the better of the other.'

A blue-green star high in the sky, dangerously green and flashing in the fields of air, made me realise my aloneness. There is much happiness in doing a task in company, in friendship, more or less silently. As each peeled wand fell to the floor, it seemed to bring nearer the summer days and nights when the baskets would be in use.

A man leans over to drop his pot into water so thick it is a painted sea, hardly stirred enough to lip the orange cliffs on whose dove-like calm kittiwakes nest: or he heaves it up from a black and silver

armoury of vicious waves at dawn, his coat gleaming with cruddled salt and phosphorus.

Varicoloured scenes; gifts of memory and of anticipation. The back of the mountain, dusty violet with masses of sea-pink and vernal squills. A spring night, the ringed moon, the sea with a sheen on it. The only way to describe that ocean is to call it muscular. On a night such as this a man might kill a dragon coiled on rocks at the foot of a dark tower; or a fugitive might sail into the haven, with a following wind out of Ireland.

There were dark thoughts, rooted in nightmare and the untrusting mind. I asked myself whether happiness could come to me here; whether it was wise in relation to my work, to my future life, to cut myself off from the outside world. I had done it once before, with disastrous results.

Now I proposed to do it in an even more uncompromising way. I wondered whether Paul was as prepared as he thought for this revolutionary change which for him would be far more novel than for me. Could we pull together like strong rowers or would we fall apart as so many others had done before us?

There is no shelter anywhere from this cold: my thoughts make me even more cold. The tide leaps past the rocks as if on an unspeakable errand to the limits of the globe.

The waves talk hurriedly and hugely of death by drowning.

Today, I struck a glass accidentally with my fork. It rang with a clear bell-like sound. A sailor struggled for life, the waves tore greedily at his flesh. I put my fingers hastily to the glass and silenced the bell, finding unbearable the eye of a doomed sailor.

A father and son (pieces broken from the rock-face) are fishing in the pale-washed light off the mountain. The grizzled father pays out the rope of the freshly-baited basket; stops the engine, and sculls over to the rocks. He puts the lad ashore. The child's form is immediately lost into the stone.

I press my finger firmly against the glass, to stop the delicate reverberation.

I I

A powerful swell was still running after the gales; the flying spray drenching Paul who sat in the bows, sheltering me behind his back. When we had been for some time in the tide-way, the tiller and the rudder fell overboard. The boat described a circle, was caught sideways by the long swells; was thrown floundering, into the troughs between. Cadwaladr, in shirt sleeves despite the biting frost, was half-way over the stern. It seemed hours before he had secured the rudder and we were again able to make a cunning track through the labyrinths of the ebb.

From the sea, the village looked even more dead than at the beginning of the freeze-up.

Dread sea; tenanted by rotting bones; furnished from wrecked vessels. Sea: on which we rocked, on which we rode, the dark tide bearing us along.

The island, black and smoked in spray, receded.

We heard the powerful, far-off throbbing of an engine. A motor torpedo-boat was coming up fast from the south east, plunging and bucking like a grey horse. It grew from a pinpoint to a trim naval corvette. It ran parallel to us though some distance off, contracted to a pinpoint again, then headed in to the shore. We were of different worlds; our craft was slow and crudely built; we sat exposed to all weathers. The torpedo-boat was built for great speed and efficiency, her crew securely cabined.

The vessel lay at anchor off-shore when we came into the bay. Cadwaladr said, 'Shall we hail her?'

So we took a turn roundabout, and the crew came on deck to stare down at us. Cadwaladr wondered if any of the crew had letters to post, or if any of them wanted to go ashore. While they telegraphed for permission to land, we rode alongside, secured to her by a rope flung from her deck. The two boats lolled towards one another and away like friendly drunkards. Our wet clothes clung, numbing us. A few of the crew stepped down into the boat. They had the pinched neurotic look of those who are no longer sailors but engine-slaves on the sea. With abnormal speed, they dash from here to there and back again. Jauntily, they knock back drinks at the bar of the hotel and talk of heavy weather from which they turned back just now down south. They don't need to fight things, to ride out storms.

The land, when we moved through it on our way back to the snow-bound village in the hills, presented a stark grey face. The sky presaged snow and a more rigid frost. It was out of the ice of this winter that we would grow the flower of a new life.

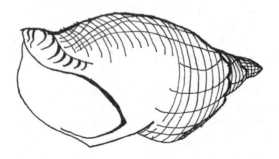

FOUR

DEEP SOUNDINGS

I

AND shall we inhabit stars? Which among the light-antennae shall house me in the dark? Who knows whether after death we shall be able to find one another in the pathless fields of black and gold?

Lathers broke on the beach, where we were alone with the evening fishers, screaming terns that, scimitar-winged, quartered the bay.

The planet Jupiter was burning in the east. All the other shiners in the heaven were pale, pallidly setting over the summer sea.

Today, we became islanders.

2

We lived at first in Ty Bychan where I had stayed alone for a short time the previous summer. It was our home from the spring of 1947 to the autumn of the following year.

We were poor, and we had at first no land except a garden, for at that time though houses were empty, every acre of earth was held between three families.

The novelty of our new life was compensation for much hardship.

The Tomos Bullnecks were at first, but only for a short time, our stay and stand-by. Owain helped us to master the practicalities of our new way of life; teaching me how to make bread; showing Paul how to skin a rock-fish by nailing it to a piece of wood and tearing off the skin with a pair of pincers to reveal the greenish flesh of the succulent fish. Cadwaladr was proud to instruct me in the art of making crab-paste; pounding the cooked meat while still hot with butter, salt, and a little vinegar.

The kitchen was a gloomy and uncomfortable room, facing the north; the oven was in the darkest corner. One day, while I was baking, Paul brought home a young raven as a pet; it took as its perching-place, the warm oven door, and snapped at me each time I

passed. It gave a half-strangled croak, and I looked carefully at it—
it was not a young raven, but a carrion crow.

Though we arrived on the island in May of 1947, it was not until
late autumn that the last of our furniture arrived, having been
brought over, a chair, or a bed, or a cupboard at a time, at Cadwaladr's
convenience. The heavy kitchen chest of drawers contained my
private papers and manuscripts. As need for them arose, I would
describe them to Owain, and he unfailingly knew exactly where to
find the papers. By going through the drawers many times he
eventually knew where everything was in detail. Nothing was lost
or broken on the way over, despite the poor state of Cadwaladr's
boat and his habit of crossing when the seas were rough.

We bought a newly-built fishing dinghy from an old boatbuilder in the village. She was a seven-foot-six dinghy, broad in the
beam and light as a storm petrel. We named her L'hirondelle and we
quickly grew to love and trust her. To propel her, we bought a
four horse-power engine, an outboard, and we began the hazardous
adventure of fishing for lobster, crayfish, and crab. Having invested
in six lobster creels, we first soaked them in the shallow waters of the
Cafn, and then in trepidation and with shaking nerves took them out
into deeper water to begin the strange search for holes where the
shellfish lurk.

An experienced lobsterman like Jacob, and he was a master at his
craft, had a deep and intimate knowledge of sea-depths right round
the island; so that he knew exactly where to drop his pots for the
best returns. We were hit or miss tyros; at first, it was rare for a
lobster to be found at the bottom of our traps. The currents in their
amazing complexity baffled and sometimes frightened us, and it was

with a sinking heart that I took the boat almost on to the cliff-foot, so that Paul could lean outboard to hook up the lobster line.

Now, these years later, it is a cause for laughter when the boat is sucked almost on to the rocks in the back-pull of a roller. The man, the boat, the rock, the wave, and the lobster have reached a true relationship, and one knows how close to shave a sea-chance.

The problem of obtaining sufficient meat for the baiting of lobster pots was a constant preoccupation, for at that time we had no trammel net to put down in the bay for bait. Paul laid snares and traps for rabbits in the mountain, the only free land there was at that time. At once, there was a sign of trouble from Cadwaladr who, now we were islanders had begun to show that he had two sides: one for the visitor, one for the neighbour, and this side was ugly and pregnant with danger. When Paul put his snares on runs that led through a wall into a field of Cadwaladr's, he was accused of taking the bread and butter out of the mouth of Cadwaladr and his family. So Paul took out his gun and spent almost the whole day on the mountain shooting rabbits. Jacob was generous to us at this time; when he had had a good haul from his nets, he would give rock-fish or a conger eel to us for bait.

For our pains, the return was pitifully small; and I having suddenly had enough potting to last me a lifetime, and realising that Paul was already showing signs of becoming a good seaman which meant that he would soon be capable of going alone round his pots as only an expert does in his young days, retired on to the land thankfully, and became the housewife again. At this time also, we became friendly with Dai. He fished alone normally, but now he sometimes took Paul with him and he began to show him a certain number of proved lobster holes; to instruct him in the vagaries of the currents, and generally to initiate him into the mysteries of his new calling. From this time, Paul's confidence increased; he began to go out to sea in all weathers, and I was constantly afraid for him; staring through the studio window to see him standing in the tiny boat appear and disappear in the strong tideway as he made his way back from the west side.

How I had grown to hate his long rubber thigh-boots because, wearing them, he would have no chance of survival in the sea, if by ill-luck, he was swept overboard.

In early September, the inevitable happened: there was a disastrous gale, in which among much general damage, our six pots broke from their ropes and were never seen by us again. Gritting our teeth, we planned to have more pots for the next season.

Despite poverty, the first winter was full of novelty for us. Paul made a draught board from a piece of paper on which he drew squares, and we used coins as counters, so that in the evenings we could play an alternative game to the eternal Whist or Patience. Sometimes we read aloud to one another in front of the driftwood fire; or on rare occasions, visited our neighbours.

Having fallen more and more under Cadwaladr's displeasure, and realising at long last that we had had his friendship at the price of lost liberty of movement and thought and privacy, we began to make tentative approaches to the other islanders; and found to our surprise that they were mild, long-suffering men and women who had been amusedly and cynically waiting for us to see the light with regard to Cadwaladr, and to turn to them. We were simply following the pattern that had already been formed by many before us; the stranger was courted and encouraged to settle on the island by Cadwaladr. Then, once he was lulled and confident and installed, Cadwaladr would begin the vendetta, until the newcomer was either driven off, or into the arms of the other islanders. Since those early days, I have seen the pattern repeated many times. Thus, a state of feud was handed down almost without variation except in the nature of the participants, from year to year.

It is possible that more than one island woman in the heat of feud, in deep secrecy may have modelled a crude image of the hated Cadwaladr; stuck pins in his vital parts and cursed his name, before throwing the doll into the consuming fire.

The roots of feud (men we had never known, many of them already dead, had been at the fount) as far back as we could trace, had started on the mainland beach, and were concerned with the island boat. Cadwaladr had tried to load a heifer on to the communal boat, but had been prevented by one of the old islanders, a venerable, larger-than-life forerunner, who had upped with a spade and threatened to brain him if he came any nearer. From that beginning, our present state of tension somehow emanated; grew and changed and intensified.

The island boat was a juicy bone between Cadwaladr and the others for many years; any plan towards communal living or a boat run as a joint venture roused the island to fever. When, as in the case of the island boat, she had a doomed and disastrous character of her own, there was certainty of trouble. A fine strongly-built sea-worthy craft, with a rakish roll on her, a sort of drunken grandeur; she was not content to be merely perverse but seemed sentient with the power of making devilish plots to discomfit the men who sailed in her. To cross the Sound there and back, was too like existence, she must live and try out ever-new forms of sea-trickery. She had a tall and cumbersome spar. For no reason at all except one felt by her own devilish choice, the mast was always mounted though the lug-sail might be left behind. On a greased-pole calm, she would be set on course; and immediately, she would begin rolling, the spar dragging her over, this way and that way, in transports of loneliness. Her ancient engine was her genius-card; it relied on careful priming of many little cups before it would even think of warming up. When, reluctantly, it consented to beat with life, the noise was horrific, with black smoke pouring from the engine casing; the boat went into the offing always to the lamentation and foreboding of those women left behind. More than once, she went on fire; at the back of the mountain when a host of men and women and children were on board; and another time, in our days, when Paul and Jacob had undertaken to man her for a trial run. Hoping for a pleasant day of rest, I went along for the sake of the trip. The engine beat like a bursting heart the whole way across the Sound until as we were drawing out of the tideway, it groaned and shuddered and rattled to a stop. It was restarted; and as if reduced to fury by the interference of the men, would only go at topmost speed. It heated rapidly; clouds of stinking fumes enveloped the engine and threatened to choke us. The men stood it for as long as it was safe; then with difficulty managed to stop it. Fortunately, a boat had not long passed us, heading in to the island; I climbed on to the combing and signalled to the other boat with a scarf, hoping to catch the eye of someone in her. After some time, they noticed we were adrift; the boat turned round, and we were towed back the way we had come.

When the boat was finally sent away to be sold because we refused to put to sea in so flighty a vessel, a fresh cause of feud was not long in arising. Land boundaries, straying sheep and cattle, chance gossip repeated with artful embellishments, inflamed the hot blood of the islanders.

3

We were insignificant as the gulls, living almost as anonymously as they. We gathered their eggs for the evening's omelette, or for putting down in water-glass against the coming winter. We would collect a few dozen at a gathering, mostly in the rocks around the seal cave. Once, at this time, one of our dogs went off by itself along a narrow ridge; he returned with an egg held most gently between his jaws. He laid it unbroken at Paul's feet.

A baby seal born in the east gut at the south end was visited daily by one or other of us, but he remained wild and fiercely watchful. At this age he was helpless and could easily have been clubbed to death. To gentle overtures of friendliness he made no response, but would become on the instant of our approach all claws, teeth and writhing body. Quick as a snake, for his seeming helplessness, he shook with aggression. How I longed to take him in my arms, to take him home with me.

Paul had rushed back from fishing with the news that there was a baby seal in the rocks.

He bit at our sea-boots and finally became so angry that he tore his own face with sharp black claws. In a few months' time, having become a confident swimmer, he would follow our boat, fearless in the freedom of the seas.

4

I baked my first bread, and marvelled at the working of the yeast, at the faint hum of its rising on the hob, at the leavening of the dough; and at the hollow sound of a well-baked loaf, the good smell of it. There was life in bread.

Bad dreams had left me. In the darkest days of the winter, on the mainland we had brooded over the map, poring over the speck of land out in the sea.

Was it real? Would we ever be there? It was so far, it was not realisable; some malevolent fate would prevent our going. I had become discouraged. Paul believing more firmly than I, had never lost his belief in the reality of the future.

The days passed quickly, with endless labour; putting the derelict house in order; distempering, painting doors and windows and floors; in the evening we played cards, Dai and Owain turning in after lobstering; bringing the sea with them into the room on their salt-stiff clothes. They played fanatically, swearing with rage and delight.

Dai, who in daily life was thoughtless to the point of folly, when playing Banco for pennies, had the most miserly regard for his imaginary riches, while the timid Owain gambled with and delighted to lose hundreds of non-existent pounds. Perhaps it was not as surprising as it appeared at first sight; for the ingenuous Owain had no appreciation of the value of money since his father made him work without wages; while Dai was an independent fisherman hoping soon to marry and to become a family man; he was always carefully counting the money in his purse.

The men slapped their thighs and laughed crazily. Outside, the green island lay in the long light of the west.

'It would be a shame for a boat to break the mirror-glass of the sea on a night like this,' said Dai, glancing through the window.

'A shame for a boat to break the skin of the sea.' More shame, that under an appearance of calm, troubles ran, currents whose power we could not assess because they ran so deep and strong and hidden.

It was with the utmost difficulty that I began to adjust myself to life on an island. For ten years I had lived in a poor mountain village, in a slate-quarrying community, with a thirty-mile stretch of open country at my back. There had been freedom in the hills; it had only been necessary to open the mountain gate and walk or ride for a whole day in wild valleys or on lonely ridges, in happy solitude.

Life on a small island I had found out at once and had been horrified at the discovery is almost entirely public so far as one's outside movements are concerned. There was almost no privacy;

wherever one went, one was watched, usually through a telescope.

One time, sleep having overcome me, I lay down in a corner of the rocks.

Next day, I was told with malicious triumph:

'You were sleeping in such and such a place yesterday, at a certain time; I saw you through the spy-glass; and I came to see what you were doing there. You were fast asleep in such and such a position. Ha! You didn't see me, but I saw you!'

Of such minute items, of such small triumphs, a man could weave the web of his days.

5

Owain was sowing corn seed in a field at the sea's edge. From where I stood in a little hollow in the heart of the island, he was a priest making sacrificial and propitiatory offering, for he seemed to be flinging out with one hand seed on to the earth, but with the other to be fertilising and placating the sea.

6

Hordes of small field-mice took up residence in the kitchen and dairy of Pant, in an openly cynical fashion, and began to waste the supplies. Nans had to resort to hanging baskets containing her butter on the iron hooks in the ceiling.

Behind the simple development of Paul's and my life together ran the shadow of mounting hatred between Nans and Cadwaladr. A blackness followed us into our dreams at night, and lay across our hearts on waking. It flung us astounded from our beds.

There was a sound of inhuman sobbing outside the door. It was Nans.

'Murder! Murder! Come quickly. Cadwaladr is killing Dai Penmon.'

Outside, there was no killing; only the after-breath of something unspeakable. The old man foaming at the lips like a rabid dog, stood cursing and waving his arms in the face of Dai. The young fisherman was smiling tightly, and blaspheming as hard as Cadwaladr. At the same time he was dabbing at his left cheek as if he had received a blow there. His hand was trembling; so that we knew his reckless laugh was partly bravado.

Cadwaladr, when he saw us, swung away up the path, and we were left with Nans, Myfanwy, and Dai. Nans was sobbing; but then, she had been sobbing off and on for weeks, and so we scarcely noticed her; it was Dai who impressed us by his silence and tenseness. Nans wiped away her tears and blew her nose into her coarse apron. Myfanwy was white and shaking, but she said nothing, only looked with dilated eyes at Dai. He picked up a cardboard suitcase from where it lay in the grass, and began to walk away down the island.

'He has turned Myfanwy out of the house,' whimpered Nans. 'And he wouldn't let her have any breakfast; he is a devil, and not a man.'

In the middle of the morning, Nans and Myfanwy and Dai went down towards the Cafn, for Myfanwy was going to the mainland with Jacob and Sion. They looked so happy and buoyant walking away along the path, that a stranger would not have known that anything had happened. The girl was laughing at Dai; and Nans had her head up, a good sign with her; and she was carrying packages, butter and eggs, I suppose, smuggled out of the house while the ogre was not looking.

(In Myfanwy's handbag was a desperate letter from Nans to her brother and sister, saying she could endure no more of her husband's cruelty. In the handbag also, was a small purse full of sovereigns.)

'For God's sake help me. I can endure no more. I'll have the law on him.'

For close on thirty years Cadwaladr had terrorised the islanders; no man or woman had ever been seized by the idea of attempting to break his spell of tyranny. For years, not one of us had set foot on his land though he, as a mark of deliberate provocation, tramped constantly over our fields and through our farm yards. As the whim took him he would invent 'ancient trackways' which he said were on the old maps, cunning paths that gave him an excuse for walking along carefully fenced banks as near to our houses as possible. Watching him helplessly, he became in our eyes the embodiment of invincible devilry until he grew bigger than life in the glory of putting so much fear into us.

It fell to Paul to break the web of dread that had laid its curse over the lives of so many people who had tried to live here and had been broken by the mad scheming of the old man. The web was broken in a mixture of mirth and rage in which we all participated.

It was the spring sheep-gathering of our third island year. We were up before the dawn and broke fast, yawning and sighing as we ate, as if crushed by the black weight of the hill-side.

We listened at the back door in the still darkness for the whistling and barking to begin.

Morning came with a soft flowing of grey vapour. In the wan light slowly spreading across the fields, we started for our stations on the cloud-invisible ridge. One of the dogs caught a rabbit just inside the mountain gate. I ran home with it and hung it in one of the out-houses (where it was forgotten until it was too bad to eat; so it was given to the Little Owl who dragged it about the floor in an ecstacy.)

I overtook Rhiannon and Eira, and we went to our places a little below the shoulder of the mountain on the west-side. The men and dogs had already disappeared over the steep eastern slopes. They were down among the boulders; Jacob, Dici Longshanks, and Paul.

The gaining sun threw beside each of us a green image of ourselves, quite unlike a noontide shadow or a mooncast ghost; and yet it was not the Brocken Spectre, the shape cast by the sun on bright drops of early morning mist and that flings a huge haloed figure out into the air.

A bitter dawn wind shook green and gold-eyed dew from the

grasses and reeds. Far below, the farms were sending up coils of wood-smoke.

The first sheep began to spill over the ridge out of cloud; worming their way in small companies between the crags. Our dogs ran back and fore to keep them from breaking back the way they had been driven. A faint bleating slowly grew into the full wail of a flock in motion. From the shelter of pockets of rock and high protecting fern in the gullies; in growing numbers they streamed from east to west. The mainland peaks stood clear in the full light of morning.

There was shining and joy; the flash of the clean night-washed sky, a gladness on the warm wind. We three women were half-way along the side of the slope towards the south and had our sheep moving towards Jacob's mountain gate which led to his stackyard, when we were suddenly confronted by Cadwaladr and Siani and Tudur, each armed with lumps of rock. Before them, they were driving the sheep we had with some difficulty gathered from the north face. Seeing us, Cadwaladr pressed the sheep more fiercely forward, so that they were more afraid of the man behind than they were of the women in front; they only hesitated a moment, then burst past us and scattered towards their grazing ground in the north. Eira, with flashing eyes and streaming hair, rushed up to the crest of the hill: standing in a prominent position, she screamed to her father that he should leave the sheep and come at once.

The men's bodies were already in a swimming heat; it needed only a small event to inflame their exasperated nerves. In heroic fashion, they toiled to the top of the ridge and without pausing for breath stormed like border raiders on to the unsuspecting Cadwaladr. Before he knew what was happening, he found himself driven back towards Ty Draw and the little gate off the mountain. Siani had by this time melted away as if into the ground; Tudur held aloof. Cadwaladr retreated slowly backwards until, tripping over a trailing bramble, he fell on his back in the hedge. The Longshanks bent down and with a gesture tore a strip from the old man's ragged waistcoat, the precious one he always kept warm in the back of the oven. Dic held up the cloth in triumph as if it had been a flag captured from the enemy. With raised sticks the men advanced upon the fallen one but he, ever quick in his reactions, squirmed on the ground and sprang upright escaping their blows; like a rat he got away through

the gate and with an astonishing speed for one of his age started to run in the direction of the lighthouse. Tudur followed him, and the lad was pursued by the three men. To give his father a good start, Tudur threw a handful of gravel full in the face of Jacob; the three flung themselves on the son and gave him a beating; then Paul, remembering the real quarry, shouted:

'Get the pants off him,' and set off on the long path to the south end. As for Eira, Rhiannon and me, we sat on the hill-side and cheered our men on, beating the earth with sticks and enjoying a good view of the race.

Siani had disappeared in the disconcerting way she shared with her old blind dog.

Meanwhile, Cadwaladr ran on, closely pursued by Paul as far as the rocks of the south end, where he hid himself and where Paul could not find him.

The other men posted themselves patiently in the tight neck of the narrows to cut off his passage homewards.

After an hour or two of skulking in his hideout, Cadwaladr the ever-dramatic even in total defeat, hobbled slowly, playing the lame old man sorely persecuted, towards the narrows. He had taken off his shirt and had mounted it on a stick as a truce-flag.

Coming up to Jacob and Dici, he said, 'SOS, I crave sanctuary. Go up and get the King, so that he can give me safe-conduct home.'

The King, who had been drinking heavily the night before, and had been snoring in bed during the trouble, now bestirred himself. This was the new King, as great a drinker as the one who had swum away.

The King showed little interest in the battle, being more full of an adventure of his own.

'Last night,' he told the emissary, the Ancient Mariner; 'a mouse got inside my nightshirt. Down the back, it was; so I pressed hard against the head of the bed, and squashed it flat as a board.'

The King then told the Ancient Mariner that the men should let Cadwaladr return home unmolested.

'Nans will be ill with worrying about what has happened to him,' he said, with a sly smile.

It was not until the next morning that we heard the news that while we had been driving the mountain on the previous day, a young fisherman from the mainland had been drowned at about the time we were making our way along below the ridge. It was the culminating tragedy in a string of misfortunes. During the previous summer Hopkyns Jones and his father had fished for lobster around the island.

Their home was on top of a steep sea-cliff on the opposite coast. They had already lost two boats to the sea. The second had been a stout crabber with two masts and a deck-house, and they had painted her green, the colour of disaster. On the day before a sudden night-gale destroyed her, she had lain becalmed hour after halcyon hour off the western islet, her red sail unmoving, a phantom in the glassy calm.

For this fishing season of 1958, Hopkyns Jones in no wise discouraged had bought a small fishing boat with the compensation money received for the loss of the other one. Now he had almost a hundred lobster pots in the sea around the island and in the Sound, a forest of green pennons flying as marker-buoys. On this fair brisk

morning while we were far above him not seeing him, he and his
boat disappeared beneath the tide. It being the time of Spring Tide,
the mystery was, why should an experienced lobsterman have
decided to force his way through the boiling waters of the north
point against the flood?

I made a drawing of Owain swimming, but it became against my
will an unknown man about to drown.

The next day, we gathered the mountain once again. I lagged behind
to keep an eye open for a rearguard action. I sat in a hollow place
among ferns, and saw Cadwaladr and Tudur moving aimlessly in
their stackyard. Cadwaladr was carrying a gun; the sunshine shone
on the barrel. It was, after all, a mere gesture; they remained the
whole day in their own part of the island.

The sting had been drawn out of Cadwaladr's tail, at least as far as
other families went. From that time on, he never again showed his
hand openly; preferring to work in subterraneous ways more
suited to his genius.

After the flock had been penned, the rest of the morning went in
separating the ewes from the lambs, until the pens were thick with
mud and dung. The ewes were then driven to the washing place in
the rocks, while the lambs awaited the return of their dams in the
evening.

From the washing, the sheep gathered on the bank, standing between us and the low sun that hung for a sad instant on the sea-rim. Shaking water from their heavy fleeces, they sprayed the air with cascades of shining drops. Each spot of water as it fell heavily, took an eye of cold light from the sun. It seemed that the wool was hung with icicles, that unearthly radiance stood about each animal.

Jacob knows each ewe in his flock by sight. He will look at her with eyes half-shut and wide-open mouth. In a trance-like voice he will give her life-history, and the history of her mother. Money and lobsters make up life to him: he has no real interest in anything else in the world.

8

Up at Pant from this day, the tension grew. Nans and Cadwaladr stalked one another like animals; she crouched into herself, the years of burning hatred and love a hump on her back; he following at a distance aware that the community was against him. She told what was happening in detail; he spoke to no one.

Dai Penmon said to us, 'I've had enough. Everything is spoilt here for me. I'm too much involved in all this trouble; Myfanwy and I are engaged to be married.'

I asked, 'Does Cadwaladr know?'

'No, but Nans does; and perhaps Cadwaladr guesses. Anyhow, I'm off this evening. Cadwaladr is following me about everywhere; even when we are out fishing, he comes too near to my boat. I think he'd like to have the courage to run me down. And he's always spying through the window at me in the evenings, to find out what I am doing. Let me look in the tide-book, so I'll know when to leave the Cafn.'

'But what work will you do? Won't you be lost away from the island? Dai, we shall miss you so.'

'I'll soon get a job, and I can find lodgings near the harbour; that way, I shan't be so far away from the sea. Myfanwy is working in a farm outside the town. In the evenings we'll go out fishing together.'

And still he delayed, though Cadwaladr was after him the whole time, keeping a close eye on his movements.

Meanwhile, nobody visited the farm of ill-fortune. It was too deranged a household. Each evening, the sun went down on their wrath, an orange yolk, a gull's egg dropping into the milky sea. Every morning, it rose in a cloudless sky, finding them ready to do battle. Nans threatened to leave, but did not go; until we despaired of any culmination short of murder.

9

At last Dai went, broken under the strain of the silent vendetta. There were only a few of us in the Cafn to see him go, for the islandmen were away on the mainland.

Tudur, in a long black overcoat a scarecrow might have been ashamed to wear, appeared beside us, his smile tucked under one ear.

'Hey,' he shouted with a gay laugh. 'You've forgotten the crabs in your storepot.' And he ran off and returned with a sack of shellfish which he shook out on to the beach. Dai selected the finest of them and gave one to each of us as parting gifts.

He, who had seemed so heedless of danger that he had become a sort of legend to us, for he had been dauntless in rowing his tiny boat over steep and running seas, now the moment had come for hi:n to leave the island for ever, expressed a superstitious fear, half genuine, half put on.

'It's an awfully small boat to cross the Sound in, isn't it,' we said. 'A bit dangerous.'

'Ay,' he agreed. 'Bloody dangerous, and what if I drown? It would be just my luck to get drowned the last time I cross the Sound.'

'Don't talk in that way,' said Rhiannon, shrewishly. 'It isn't lucky.'

Dai jumped into his boat, and went out into the bay. Rhiannon shook her head and gave a shiver.

'It's a very small boat.'

We waved him godspeed with both arms, as the custom is with us.

As he reached Pen Clogwyn, Jacob's boat swept through foam to pass him. Good-byes were shouted; we saw their raised arms. Farewell!

Somewhere behind, around the back of the mountain, Cadwaladr too must be returning home, but from him there would be no glance of recognition.

10

The next morning, Nans in her best black coat and hat, walked away from her home for what she had decided should be the last time, while her men were out fishing.

But where were the two youngest children? Surely, she would not leave them with their father? She was carrying a big cardboard box tied with rope. When I greeted her, she barely glanced at me. Her face was ghastly, a sick yellow, and fixed in a grimace.

She went down to Rhiannon's and hid there.

When Owain came up from fishing, Jacob met him by the boat-house and told him that his mother was in Ty Draw with Rhiannon and that he was to join her there. Owain, blank as a board, said, 'Very well,' and wandered up the lane as if this was a day like any other day, and not the turning point of his life.

Cadwaladr, suspecting nothing, went home for dinner, driving Siani before him with a stick as was his custom, like a beast to the slaughtering pen.

He realised what had happened when he found the house empty and no food prepared. He went to Ty Draw, his arms beating the air in a fury of intention. He stumped into Jacob's kitchen and ordered Owain to come home for his meal.

'No,' said Owain; 'no, I'm going away with my mother.'

'To hell with you both, then; but the young ones stay by me.'

The father and his youngest children looked for maggoty sheep while Jacob took the runaway mother and son across the Sound. Doglike, the children ran at their father's heels. No shadow of awareness, nothing but the completest indifference was on their faces, for they had learned early the use of the mask.

Eyeing the strongly running tide in the Sound, Cadwaladr said, as if it was something that only remotely touched him, this running away of his woman and elder son,

'They've gone a bit early on the tide. It'll be dirty on the headland for them.' Then, with detachment he added:

'Maybe they were afraid I'd go over before them and get there first and bring them back.'

The five of us; the children, Cadwaladr, Paul and I, sat on the upturned boat under which hens roost. We sheltered from the sun in the shadow of the ruin, and in the shade of the stone Christus racked on the granite cross.

Sweet sense of liberation! O relaxation of nerves. Nihil ad vos? O viatores omnes.

It was a full month before any trace was found of Hopkyns Jones and his boat, apart from a floating bait-box and a broken oar. At the month's end his boat was found drifting in the bay not far outside the Cafn. A week later, his body was washed ashore thirty miles away on the shore of the Great Bay.

I I

Immense night had relaxed its hold on the muscular sea; leaving the water lithe as a snow-leopard. The light was strong as it is on the east coast of Scotland; the same brilliance, the same clean air. The earth gave me a sense of comfort, with the ground so warm, the atmosphere dry.

While lobstering round the island we saw at Maen Bugail that there were about fifteen seals lying on the rocks above spray level. A cow and her white, jet-eyed pup swam round the boat. As we approached, those seals that had not already dived into the sea, reared on their flippers to look at us. One after the other, they moved over the rocks like slugs and splashed into the water. The last to leave was twice as broad as any of the others, and he was the mottle-backed king of the herd. He snorted, with quivering nostrils, and dived. Whiskered faces bobbed up round the boat, with outstretched necks.

We dragged without success with a cluster of iron hooks at the end of a long rope for a lost lobster pot. The sea was densely clouded.

My mind is battered by warnings now that we own a boat and are beginning to fish for lobster.

'Never go to sea without an anchor, in case you get into trouble when you are fishing. A big rock, and a sufficient length of rope, will do. Chip a waist in the middle of it so the rope won't slip off . . . Be careful where the wreck lies in the bay. You might drop your anchor through an open hatchway and get stuck . . .'

I 2

Jacob works in the hay-meadows like one possessed. When the other men and the women have gone up to the house for dinner at the summons of the conch-shell, he goes on steadily; seated on the rattling machine behind the old white mare who is slow and timid of the soft marshy field. Her feet flounder among half-sodden hay, and the weight of the machine holds her back. The hay-forks, as they strike out, toss the hay like monstrous iron claws of a robot fowl. Where the ground is too soft Jacob turns the heavy swathes by hand.

I 3

Eira saved my life on the east side; it is a strange thing, but it happened many times when there was danger on the island; it would be our two selves facing it.

This was the way of it. Jacob had asked me to give a hand to catch

a few sheep that had strayed on to the back of the mountain. There were only the three of us free that morning; Jacob, Eira, and me. Four sheep had gone astray and they must be caught for shearing. We caught three among the rocks and Jacob hobbled them. The fourth was one of the devil's own; determined not to be taken. It was a fine warm morning and she soon had us in a lather of sweat; she kept low, taking to the cliffs.

She ran out over the cliff where the shags nest, and being pressed by the dogs, leapt out towards the waves, landing head foremost on a shelf of naked rock. We thought she must have broken her neck or at the very least, her nose; but not this ewe! She scrambled up, ran along the foot of the stone, and getting round the rocks where we could not see her, came up the grass quietly behind us and began to make for the mountain crest. I went mad then; the sweat running down into my eyes. We were on the steepest part of the east side, and it being a time of great drought the earth was almost bare and treacherous as silk. I had begun to claw my way up after the ewe when one of the dogs overtook her and turned her round straight towards me, his mouth snapping at her hindquarters. Gritting my teeth, I vowed to catch her by the leg as she went past me, or die in the attempt; a lunatic thought, with the speed at which she was moving. At the last, the dog sank his fangs in her leg, and she leapt at me. I was half-sitting; in self-defence, turned my back to her. She hit me in full flight in the small of the spine, and by rights, I should have gone with her into the sea. Through the sickness of pain in my back, I understood that I had not moved above an inch or two, and could not guess the reason. A great weight across my buttocks was holding me nailed to the earth. When I was able to move, I looked round, to see Eira. She had seen what would happen, and had leapt across the yards that separated us, to throw her weight across me. Touching my back, my hand came away red with blood on my shirt; it was not my blood but that of the ewe, for she had damaged her nose when she fell over the shags' cliff. She was swimming below, and it was great luck that I was not there too. She came ashore, and was hobbled, and seemed none the worse; indeed, she broke her hobble even then, and made another dash for liberty before she was finally caught and shorn. As for me, I slunk home, not wishing anyone to see the thickly bloodstained shirt. My back, though tender, was not broken after all, and the blood ran out of the shirt when it was put in salt and cold water.

> Now, on a shimmering sweet siren day
> Of soft summer O lazy passionate season
> After snow has melted thawed melted blossomed
> Into red petals of prodigious roses I ask
> Where you are where you are where you are
>
> On the back porch, your old raincoat
> Crumpled and cracked from its travels
> Hangs above army boots grey with dust
> From Saint Pierre and Miquelon
>
> Come again, black days of rain and no sun
> I have had enough summer. The Chinese poets
> Point far away over drenched grasses
> Towards the distant snow mountains

A year ago today we were together
Do you remember O memory retain
A white horse passing in the mist
And how your hands were stained
With the juice of a purple fish

14

In summer, there was much humidity and sea-fog, so that nothing would be visible for whole days and nights on end.

There would be a brightness denoting the shore and the tide's edge. At times there lay between shingle and sea bleached bones of sheep that had died and been thrown over-cliff only to return as fragments of bone and wool.

About noon, returning from fishing, through unidentifiable fields, we saw the haze of luminous roofs and paused, not knowing where we had strayed. A break in the clouds showed a patch of sun-flooded earth over which Eira moved eagerly like a freed slave, behind the white horse. They were churning outside the milk-house; the horse held captive by a length of wire running from his bridle to the long shaft revolving on the head of the iron stand in the centre of the trampled circle of gravel. In the milk-house a few yards away, the slowly-forming butter in the churn connected underground with the shaft outside, thumped round: thump and splash, butter and whey.

The girl walked slowly, impatiently tossing her head; moving on the balls of her feet, a whip in her hand, she urged the old mare to keep up a steady pace. A figure in a dream, she was spun out of fog.

It had first thinned round the buildings, so that the roofs were a dim violet, the walls hallucinatory. The fog-horn still echoed down corridors of vapour. At last, the sun came through, hot and powerful, disclosing the girl where she strode tossing away the black ringlets on to her shoulders; her breasts and hips moving with virginal power. And the whole time, she scolded and quarrelled with the patient horse, driving him on with the wit of her tongue and the impatience of youth.

15

'It isn't as if you needed to live out there, in such a god-forsaken place,' said the postmaster.

'No,' I answered, on guard against anything he might say.

'It isn't as if you had been born to the life,' said the postmaster.

'No,' I said, waiting for his sentences to be laid down like baited traps. We watched one another for the next move. The man lifted a two-ounce weight from the counter and dropped it with fastidious fingers on to the brass scale. As the tray fell, I acknowledged that he had found a chink in my armour. He breathed importantly, and spread his hands on the counter. From pressure on the palms, dark veins stood up under the skin on the backs of his hands. He leaned his face to the level of my eyes.

'You'll soon get tired of it,' he rapped out. 'Have you thought what it will be like in the winter? Can you bake bread? What if you break a leg, and the sea is too rough for a doctor to get across?'

O, my God. But this doesn't really matter, I told myself. At least, it would not, once I was back on the island. It floated in front of the postmaster's face. The rocks were clear, and the hovering wind-swung birds: they stood clear in front of the wrinkles and clefts of his brow and chin. He coughed discreetly and shrugged with small deprecatory movements of the shoulders. He slid aside and faced the window.

'Seems as though it will be too risky for you to go back this evening,' he said. 'There's a bit of fog about. Will you be staying the night in the village?'

'And he wouldn't let her go on holiday in the winter: he said, if she did, he'd get a concubine to keep him warm, and he meant . . . '

A woman was talking to her friend outside the door.

'You cannot possibly cross the Sound alone in this weather,' persisted the postmaster.

'I must get back tonight, Mr. Davies.'

He sketched the bay with a twitching arm, as if to say:

'I have bound the restless wave.'

He became confidential, turning to stretch across the counter.

'My dear madam, no woman has ever before navigated these waters alone. Why, even on a calm day, the Porth Meudwy fishers will not willingly cross the Sound. Be warned, dear lady! Imagine my feelings if you were to be washed up on the beach here.'

'I am afraid it is most important that I should get back tonight, Mr. Davies.'

Ann Pritchard from the corner house slid from the glittering evening into the shadows of the post office. She spoke out of the dusk behind the door.

'It isn't right for a woman to ape a man, doing a man's work.'

'Paul is ill. He couldn't possibly come across today. That is why I'm in charge of the boat,' I answered.

Two other women had slipped in against the wall of the shop. Now, four pairs of eyes were boring into me. With sly insolence the women threw ambiguous sentences to the postmaster, who smiled as he studied the grain in the wood of the counter. I picked up my bundle of letters and prepared to go.

'The tide will be about right now. Good evening, Mr. Davies.'

'Be very very careful; and remember me to your husband.' Their laughter followed me into the street. It was like dying while crowds danced and mocked.

'O, my darling, my darling, over the cold waves.' I knew that while I was away he would try to do too much about the farm. He would go to the well for water, looking over the fields he lacked the strength to drain. He would be in the yard, chopping wood.

By the stone bridge over the river, one of the village fishermen, Griff Owen, was leaning against the side of a motor car, talking to a man and woman in the front seats.

He said to them, 'Ask her,' as I went past.

'Excuse me, could you take us over to see the island?'

'I'm sorry; there's a storm coming up. It wouldn't be possible to make the double journey.'

They eyed me, stiff with curiosity.

Griff Owen, and the grocer's boy carrying two boxes of provisions, followed me on to the beach.

'I wouldn't be you; it's going to be a dirty night,' said the man.

The waves were chopped, and the headland was vague with hanging cloud. The two small islets in the bay were behind curtains of vapour. The sea was blurred and welcomeless. To the island, the island. Here in the village, you opened a door: laughter and jokes buzzed in your face. They stung and blinded. O my love, be patient. I am coming back to you; quickly, quickly, over the waves.

The grocer's boy put down the provisions on the sand near the tide edge. Immediately, a shallow pool formed round the bottom of the boxes.

'Wind seems to be dropping,' said Griff.

'Yes, but I think there will be fog later on.' I turned to him. 'Oh, Griff, what would we do without you? You are always so kind to us.'

He laid a hand on my shoulder.

'Tell me, how is he feeling?'

'Always, when he catches cold, he runs a fever and then he starts coughing; but living in the clean air from the sea is good. Don't worry; he is hanging on to life and the island.'

We began to push the boat down over rollers towards the water. Last week, Paul had said quite abruptly as he was stirring the boiled potatoes for the ducks:

'At least, you will have this land if I die.'

At least, I will have the island.

'Well, well,' said the man, making an effort to joke, 'Tell him from me, that I'll come over to see him if he comes for me himself. Tell him, I wouldn't trust my life to a lady, even though the boat has a good engine and knows her own way home.'

'Mr. Davies coming down,' said the boy, looking over his shoulder as he heaved on the side of the boat. The postmaster came on to the beach through the narrow passage between the hotel and the churchyard. His overcoat flapped round him in the wind. The boat was floating; provisions and parcels had been stowed away. Mr. Davies came to the water's edge.

'Another letter for you,' he said. 'I'm very sorry; it had got behind the old age pension books.'

He peered, longing to know what was in the letter, dying to find out what my feelings would be when I saw the handwriting. He had already devoured the envelope with his eyes, back and front, reading the postmark and the address. He sucked in his cheeks and mumbled something. Only the grocer's boy, whistling as he kicked the shingle, did not respond to what he said. I forced myself to smile. It was like a death; every hour spent on the mainland gave fresh wounds.

'Thank you, Mr. Davies. Good-bye, Griff; see you next week if the weather isn't bad.' I climbed over the gunwale and weighed anchor; bent over the engine and it began to live.

The grocer's boy was drifting away, still kicking the beach as if he bore it a grudge.

Mr. Davies called in a thin voice, 'Great care ... wish you would ... the Sound and ... '

Griff waved, and roared like a horn, 'Tell him: I'll take the next calf if it is a good one.'

It was his way of wishing god-speed. Linking the moment's hazard to the safety of future days.

The men grew small; they and the gravestones of blue and green slate clustered round the church at the top of the sand. The village drew into itself; fell into perspective against the distant mountains. At last, the tall headstones of the churchyard looked like hosts of pilgrims waiting for a boat.

It was lonely in the bay, but there was comfort from the steady throbbing of the engine. The sea was bleak and washed of colour under the shadow of a long roll of mist that stretched from the level of the water almost to the sun. It was nine o'clock in the evening. I knew I could not reach the anchorage before ten and though it was summertime, darkness would have fallen before I had reached home.

The wind blew fresh, but the wall of mist did not seem to move at all. Would Pen Clogwyn and the mountain be visible when I rounded the cliffs into the Sound?

Soon now, I should be able to see the island mountain. I knew every islandman would sooner face a storm than fog.

The mainland, the islets, the cliff-top farms of the peninsula fell away. Porpoise rolling off-shore towards the Sound lifted my heart for their companionship.

Before entering the white silence of the barren wall of fog, I took a compass-bearing; and was immediately both trapped and free; trapped because it was full daylight and yet it was dark as if blindness had fallen over me, not blindness where everything is black, but blindness where eyes are filled with a vague light and they strain helplessly. Is it that I cannot see, is this loss of sight? The horror was comparable to waking on a black winter night and being unable to distinguish anything, until in panic one thinks, has my seeing gone? And free, because the mind could build images of mist-walls; my spirit could lose itself in tunnels of vapour.

The sound of the motor-boat's engine was monstrously exaggerated by the fog. Like a giant's heart it pulsed: thump, thump. There was a faint echo, as if another boat, a ghost ship, moved nearby. The mind had too much freedom in these gulfs.

The boat began to pitch like a bucking horse. I was made aware of depth upon depth of water underneath the boards on which my feet were braced. It was the Sound. The tide poured across my course. A brightness of cloud reared upward from the water's face. Not that it was anywhere uniform in density; high up, there was suddenly a thinning, a tearing apart of vapour with a wan high blue showing through; and once, the jaundiced weeping sun was partly visible low in the sky, which told me that I was still on the right bearing. There were grey-blue caverns that seemed like patches of land, but they were effaced by new swirls of cloud, or came about me in imprisoning walls, tunnels along which the boat moved only to find nothingness at the end. Unconsciously, I must have gritted my teeth when we ran into the fog-bank. The tension remained. Paul's ghost sat in the bows. As a figurehead, he leaned away, his face half lost in opaque cloud.

'I will get home safely. I will get home.'

The phantom persisted; it answered my spoken thought. Paul turned round, his face serious.

'When you get across the Sound, if you can hear the fog-horn,' he said quietly, 'you are on the wrong tack. If you can't hear it, you're all right. It means you are cruising safely along the foot of the cliffs . . . '

Soon, you'll be on the cold floor of the sea, said reason. Spouts of angry water threatened the boat that tossed sideways. Salt spray flew over.

'Careful, careful,' warned Paul. 'We are nearly on Pen Cader; the rocks are near now, we are almost out of the Sound.' A herring gull flapped close, then with a cry swerved away, its claws pressed backward.

Above the noise of the engine, there was now a different sound, that of water striking land. For an instant, I saw the foot of a black cliff. Wet fangs snapped at the boat. Vicious fangs, how near they were. Shaken by the sight, by the rock death that waited, I turned the boat away from the island. White foam spouted against the black and slimy cliff. I found myself once more alone. The phantom Paul, leaving me to the sea, had been sucked into the awful cloud, vapour without substance or end. I listened for the fog-horn. No sound from the lighthouse. A break in the cloud above my head drew my eyes. A few yards of the mountainside was visible, seeming impossibly high, impossibly green and homely. Before the eddying mists rejoined, I saw a thin shape trotting across the steep grass slope; far, far up near the crest of the hill. Leaning forward I forgot where I was, and cried aloud, 'O, look, the dog.' It was our sheepdog keeping watch. The hole in the cloud closed up, the shroud fell thicker than ever. It was terrible, this loneliness, this groping that seemed as if it would go on for ever.

The low-throated horn was suddenly audible, coming from somewhere on the right hand. In avoiding the rock, I had put out too far and had overshot the anchorage. I must have been somewhere off the southern headland near the pirate's rock. A line of lobster floats passed.

I stopped the engine and anchored the boat to the lobster line, hoping that the fog would clear at nightfall. There was an unnatural silence after the engine was cut out. Water knocked against the boat.

Cold seeped into my bones from the planks. With stiff wet hands I opened the bag of provisions, taking off the crust of a loaf and spreading butter on it with a gutting knife I found in the bows.

While I ate, I realized that for the first time in weeks there was leisure to review life. For on the farm, it was eat, work, sleep, eat, work, sleep, in rotation.

I asked myself, 'Have I sinned, or is happiness not for me? How have I sinned? Is too great happiness a sin? Surely, it's only because I am frightened of the fog that I ask, have I sinned, is this my punishment? When the sun shines, I take happiness with both hands. Perhaps it's wrong to be happy when half the people in the world are chain-bound and hungry, cut off from the sun. If you scratch below the surface of men's minds, you find that they are bleeding inwardly. Men want to destroy themselves. It is their only hope. Each one secretly nurses the death-wish; to be god and mortal in one; not to die at nature's order, but to cease on his own chosen day. Man has destroyed so much that only the destruction of all life will satisfy him.

How can it be important whether I am happy or unhappy? And yet, it's difficult for me to say, I am only one; what does my fate matter? For I want to be fulfilled like other women. What have I done to be lost in winding sheets of fog?

And he will be standing in the door, wondering that I do not come.

For how long had I been sitting in the gently-rocking boat? It was almost dark, and my eyes smarted from the constant gazing. Mist weighed against my eyeballs. I closed the lids for relief. Something was staring at me. The steady glance of a sea-creature. I looked over the darkening waves, an area of a few yards; beyond, the wave-crest was cloud, the cloud was water. A dark, wet-gleaming thing to starboard. It disappeared before I could make out what it was. And then, those brown beseeching eyes of the seal-cow. She had risen nearby, her mottled body scarcely causing a ripple. Lying on her back in the grey-green gloom of the sea she waved her flippers now outwards, now inwards to her white breast, saying, come to me, come to me, to the caverns where shark bones lie like tree stumps, bleached, growth-ringed like trees.

Mother seal, seal cow!

The attraction of those eyes was almost enough to draw me to salt death. The head disappeared. The dappled back turned over in the opaque water, and dived. I found myself praying that this gentle visitant should not desert me.

Hola, hola, hola, seal mother from the western cave. Come to me, come to me, come to me. The stone-grey head reappeared on the other side of the boat. Water ran off the whiskers and she showed her profile; straight nose, and above, heavy lids drooping over melancholy eyes. When she plunged, showing off her prowess, a sheen of pearly colours ran over the sleek body.

We watched one another until the light failed to penetrate the fog. After the uneasy summer twilight had fallen, I was still aware of the presence of the seal. I dozed off into a shivering sleep through which I heard faintly the snorting of the sea creature. A cold desolate sound. Behind that again was the full-throated horn bellowing into the night. From time to time, the untameable sea slopped over the gunwale to wet my feet.

I dreamt that Paul was taking me up the mountain at night under a sky dripping with blood. Heaven was on fire. Paul was gasping for breath. The other islanders came behind, their long shadows before them up the slope. The mountain top remained far off.

Out of dream, I swam to consciousness, painfully leaving the dark figures of fantasy. A sensation of swimming upwards through fathoms of water. The sea of my dreams was dark and at certain levels between sleeping and waking, a band of light ran across the waves. Exhaustion made me long to fall back to the floor of oblivion, but the pricking brain floated me at last to the surface of morning.

I awoke with a wrenching gasp that flung me against the gunwale. Wind walked the sea. The fog had gone, leaving the world raw and disenchanted in the false dawn. Already, gulls were calling for a new day. Wet and numb with cold, I looked about me. At first, it was impossible to tell off what shore the boat was lying. For a few minutes, it was enough to know that I was after all at anchor so close to land.

Having passed down the whole eastern coastline in the fog, I had rounded the south end and now lay a little way past Mallt's bay on the west side. The farmhouse, home, seemed near across the fore-shortened fields. Faint light showed in the kitchen window, a warm glow in the grey landscape.

It was too early for the other places, Ty Draw, Clogwyn, Pant, to show signs of life. Field, farm, mountain; sea and sky. What a simple world; and below, the undercurrents.

I started up the engine, and raced round to the anchorage through mounting sea-spray and needles of rain.

After the boat had been made secure against the rising wind, I trudged over seaweed and shingle, carrying the supplies up into the boathouse. It was a temptation to loiter inside the sheltering walls after putting down the bags of food. Being at last in shelter, no longer pitched and tumbled on the sea, confused the mind. Wind howled and thumped the walls. Tears of water raced down the body of a horse scratched long ago on the window by Paul. Sails stacked under the roof shivered in the draught forced under the slates. It was like spinning wildly in some wild dance. The floor rose and fell as the waves had done. The earth seemed to slide away and come up again under the feet. I leant on the window-sill, with forehead pressed to the pane. Through a crack in the glass wind poured in a cold stream. Nausea rose against returning to the shore for the last packages. After that, there would be the whole length of the island to walk.

At the tide-edge, spume blew across the rocks, covering my sea-boots with a beery scum. A piece of wrack was blown into the wet tangle of my hair. Picking up the bag of provisions, I began the return journey. Presently I stopped, put down the bag, and went back towards the surf, for I had been so long with the sea that the thought of going inland was unnerving. Wading out until the water was swirling round my knees, I stood relaxed. My face felt stiff with encrusted salt. My feet were sucked by outdrawn shingle. I no longer had the will to struggle and could have let a wave carry me beyond the world.

I wanted sleep. The sea mourned, sleep. The wind sobbed, sleep.

Oystercatchers flying in formation, a pattern of black and white and scarlet, screamed, 'We are St. Bride's birds, we saved Christ, we rescued the Saviour.'

A fox-coloured animal was coming over the weedy rocks of the point. It was the dog, shivering and fog-stained as if he had been out all night. He must have been lying in a cranny and so missed the sight of me when I had arrived. He fawned about my feet, barking unhappily.

We went home together, the dog and I, passing Ty Draw that slept: Clogwyn too. It was about four o'clock of a summer day-break. Mushrooms were glowing in their own radiance. I remembered my first morning walk on the island. There had been a green and lashing sea, and gullies of damp rock, and parsley fern among loose shale. Innocent beginning, uncomplicated, shadowless. As if looking on the dead from the pinnacle of experience, I saw myself as I had been.

When at last I opened the house-door, a chair scraped inside. Paul was standing in the kitchen, white with strain and illness.

'So you did come, after all,' he said dully.

Putting down the bags, I said, yes. How sick, how deathly, he looked.

'Really, you shouldn't have sat up all night for me.' He said, stirring the pale ashes from which rose a fine white dust: 'Look, there's still fire, and the kettle's hot.'

He coughed. We drank the tea in silence, standing far apart. However hard I tried to brace my feet, the floor seemed to lurch giddily beneath me. Paul went and sat down before the hearth. Without turning his head, he said:

'Your hair's wet. You must be so tired.'

'Yes, so tired. Almost worn out.'

Colour was slowly draining back into the world. It came from the sea, to penetrate the wild irises near the well, and the withy beds in the corner of the field.

Through the open window, came the lowing of cattle. Clogwyn cows were being driven up for milking.

16

There were subtle breaks in the pattern of feud. Cadwaladr was until the end someone with whom we would never be reconciled,

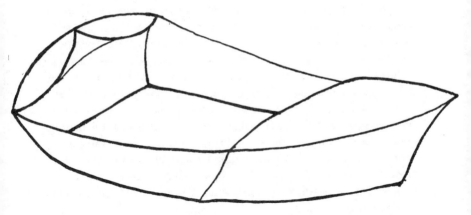

but Tudur was universally loved and even spoilt; and he had the right of entry to all our houses; Siani was strongly suspect and shunned by everyone, for she showed to an alarming degree the tricksy nature of her father.

Tudur, like his father, had been born without fear. For his own use, he had a boat of battered sheet-metal so small that he could just fit into it. The boat was flat-bottomed and shallow. In this dangerous shell he would set out on abortive attempts to kill seals with a harpoon gun; whistling, singing, and eager to risk the dangerous passage of the south end.

17

It is August, with fat stock being moved from island to mainland. Dealers with their wives and families came over early in the morning, helped to round up the sheep on the mountain, and to sort out the lambs.

On the day that we drove the flock to the sea I thought, looking at Rhiannon and Eira, at the strong light beating on the animated faces, and the sheep in a cloud of dust, that it was a pastoral uninfluenced by time. We drove the animals (they were hobbled so that they had little chance of straying) into a corner of the rocks until the boats were launched. Sweating and swearing, slipping on slimy boulders, we got the sheep into a coign in the cliff from whence the men could with ease lift them aboard. Nearly a hundred animals were packed into the black boat, and ten into the motor boat. There was scarcely any water in the gutter when we took off. The black boat was so full of sheep and water that it took time to float her, though the men made superhuman efforts to push her into the deep channel. Jacob took me, along with a gold-skinned peasant girl, the sister of Dic Longshanks, in the leading boat. From the cattle boat the bailing buckets flashed in, out, in, out; pouring streams of dirty water overboard. By a miracle she did not sink. By faith alone does that vessel cross the Sound. With her black bulk behind, the towing boat's crew might be justified in doing what men did long ago on their way across these waters. Row a little, ship oars, remove hats, pray ardently: 'O God, grant that we come in safety.' And bend again to the blades, repeating the formula until landfall was made.

The sheep were to be left at the nearest farm on the mainland until the dealer's truck came for them. We went into the close-walled cove between floats marking lobster pots. The lambs were slung out on to the shingle. The first one on shore turned its face towards the waves and in no way impeded by its hobble, swam briskly out to sea again. Bloody uffern! Sion pushed a dinghy out and rowed after the swimmer, catching it before it had reached the cove. Heat poured down. Hot untempered light burned the cove. The sheep were tired and hungry, and had no fear of us, but lay on the laneside and snatched mouthfuls of grass and flowers. Fragile harebells became entangled round their horns. Unaware that they were garlanded beasts of sacrifice, they went slowly, crying and breathing heavily, up the fisherman's track to the farm above.

In a corner of the beach below the village stood a thin figure in black. It was old Megan Prydderch, Jacob's friend who had a cottage near the river mouth where it spread out in a rapid shallow to enter the sea. Until the week of her death she kept watch for his boat. On every day that there was the possibility of his coming over from the island, she waited, staring from under the brim of her wide black hat towards the Point, sometimes looking for driftwood, and in winter tending her salmon nets. She had never been married, but for twenty years Iolo the Mill, an old cripple who worked at the smithy had lived with her. In his spare time and particularly on summer evenings, Iolo fished for mackerel in the Sound. He so cherished his boat, the only one he had ever built, it had become his child to be guarded against men and tides. Each time after it had been used, with the assistance of Megan he carried it up the low sand bank and carefully cradled it on wedges in the harsh marram grass before the door through which as he ate he could caress the beloved shape with his eyes.

18

We had to bring a drunken man, an engineer, back with us that night. He could not be persuaded to leave the bar of the hotel. Jacob's face was seamed with worry as he sat waiting in the black boat. The tide was already on the turn and he was anxious to be away.

The man, reeling and cross-eyed with drink, refused to leave beer and companions. The world was a haze of clinked glass and disembodied voices. Fog and clear pictures. A pair of eyes, glistening wet. A mouthful of laughter. Black out. The walls change places with floor and ceiling. They fall away in a flash of light that almost steadies him. Fog closes in all round. It clears. He studies the wall: sees a sampler worked in blue, green, and yellow wools, of a barque sailing to a rocky shore scarcely contained within the frame. Under the picture it says: The island from the SSW.

Ah, the mountain in the sea. What a life! He begins to weep at the thought of it.

Have you seen Eira, the rose of the wilderness? He stares hard at a face swaying near his own. He translates the face into terms of drink.

Have another? From a wad of pound notes sprayed on the counter he selects one and passes it to the bar tender.

William the barman has a blotched scarlet face from which like a root the huge nose thrusts. His eyes say: I see and record nothing. His ears, thirsty plants, drink in every word, every scrap of floating gossip. He smiles painfully like a whipped dog at his master the hotel proprietor, who sits, fresh from the bath; paunchy, sandalled, cool in a heavy silk shirt, on the half door of the bar. The master touches with tender fingers the pale bristles of an experimental moustache. He smiles back at William. The man pours out another sacrificial glass.

The engineer is angered against his will. Left alone, he would be quite happy. He does not want to feel anger. What are those fingers clutching at his arms, trying to lead him away when he is beginning to forget?

'Leave me alone,' he shouts. 'I'm not coming. Let the boat wait for me. Tell Jacob he can damn well wait for me. What do I care for the tides?'

Along the beach, Jacob sits on a thwart of the black boat. Paul comes down from the pub, shaking his head.

'Can't move him,' he says.

Sion of the long legs goes to try his luck.

Thou drunken hero: with the village as audience, the engineer came through the sand supported by Sion and the postmaster. He was held by the braces at the water's edge by Paul; lifted like a sack on to the broad shoulders of Sion, and thrown into the black boat whose bottom was swilling with foul water and rotten straw. I went aboard, scrambled along the gunwale to the bows, and passed over into the motor boat.

It was cool dusk with a fine adventurous breeze.

Fishing craft coming inshore were saluted by the drunkard, but by the time the boats were well out in the bay his imagination had dried. I saw Paul laying an oar in the bows of the black boat. He led the engineer forward. The man disappeared, having suddenly and deeply fallen asleep in the water and wet straw. Buckets of bilge-water vomited over the side.

Jacob sets a course for the bay-islets; so that in the event of engine trouble we shall have a safe distance between us and the tide rushing through the Sound. Off the point of the larger islet an eddy tide runs. The boat is pulled violently by the lurching of the cattle-boat astern. The engineer rouses himself to look round as we pass across smooth black whirlpools. Hard to starboard. A whirlpool and a stretch of broken water. Jets! Those in the boat astern are oblivious to the pull of the tide. I begin to read a letter, and Paul signals to me.

'What's your mail?'

'A long letter from Friedrich.'

What did Friedrich start, when he had the whim to bring me here?

19

Pale stars came out in the pale sky. Under the eastern heights of the mainland we could just make out a dinghy lying secured to a lobster pot. It had been in tow; the boat drawing it had not been able to make headway against the tide with the weight of the dinghy and its four Baptist minister passengers. So Twm (for it was he with two loads of trippers) had to empty his first party on the distant beach before returning in the darkness for the tethered dinghy. We, far to the westward, could barely make out the boat with its freight of angry, frightened people.

Stars grow, until shaking, they light one another's worlds.

The engineer lifts his hands to the sky, takes a drunken step, and almost falls over the gunwale. He sings a bawdy song. Water ripples, and cold bubbles run, caused by the cleaving bows. We are coming home to the rock in the darkness. The Cafn is black and deserted when the engineer staggers ashore, and from a rent in his pocket leaves a shower of silver in the bottom of the boat. He sings and waves his arms, embracing Paul.

'You beautiful singer! My wife sings too; my wife, blast her eyes for leaving me. She skinned me of everything; ruined me and left me.'

He could not tear himself away from us; he refused to go up to the lighthouse. First, he went home with the dismayed Jacob, just to say good-night to Eira.

'Give me a kiss. I've come to propose to you, Eira, in the public view of the world. Come up the mountain in the dark with me, darling. Let's go maggoting together. There's a thing or two I could teach you about love.'

We heard him down at the foot of the hill, shouting outside the Levens's house, demanding to be allowed in to say good-night and to drink the health of the family.

Then he came to us up at the north end, companioned by a dog and cat picked up on his walk. Twice he knocked at our door, thrust beer bottles on the table, and went out whistling after shaking hands and declaring we were his dearest and truest friends.

The carnation he had thrust in his buttonhole in the morning was still fresh and intact.

That night, Paul dreamt he was bailing out. He found himself sitting up in bed and going through the actions of flinging out a pail of water.

20

As soon as the business of the ram lambs was over, the fat bullocks and a young heifer or two, and a bull that had served his time among the milking herd, were transported amidst general disorder and near-accident. A day or so before the beasts were to be taken away, long ropes were attached to their horns and allowed to trail on the ground behind, thus making the animals easier to handle. On the day of embarkation, two steers were selected and driven towards the sea. In hedge-gaps along the way we women and children posted ourselves to head them off. One animal was so nervous that it made many bids for freedom, throwing itself on to the high banks oblivious of barbed wire, gorse bushes, and thickets of bramble. It splashed its way through the swamps followed by the Longshanks and Jacob; it was forced to return torn and bloody, its tongue hanging out dry and quivering. No sooner was it on the long flat land above the anchorage than it made a last supple plunge for freedom. Dic Longshanks had wound the end of the rope round his arm. The bullock took him off-balance, pitching him forward on to his face. Tenacious of the rope, he was dragged full-length along the ground. The devil-may-care Dic was not dismayed but continued to laugh; leaping up and throwing weight on to his heels, to act as a brake upon the runaway. The panting half-maddened animal was at last led down towards the boat and made to walk up the ramp—a hatch-cover placed on boulders.

With its high slatted sides, the cattle-boat resembled a roofless ark. The bullock's foreleg was lifted up over the gunwale by Jacob, while Rhiannon and the King and Levens pulled strongly on a rope across the beast's buttocks to force the hindquarters towards the boat's side. No sooner was the beast amidships than Jacob had him tied by the head to the hurdle bolted on the forward thwart. As the men were about to slip a pole along the steer's flank to act as a barrier between it and the other animal that was to follow, there was a flash of sheet-lightning followed on the instant by a clap of thunder. The beast now utterly unnerved drew together every reserve of strength and reared up, loosening the head-ropes. Its forefeet plunged between the slats of the hurdle while it stabbed the decking with its hindlegs.

'There is no holding it.'

Jacob was in a ferment for the safety of his boat. At any moment a plank might be stoved in.

'It is the thunder,' Paul shouted at him.

From the shadow of the Cormorant, Cadwaladr had been watching us, a Cheshire grin about his eyes. Jacob in this crisis had become as frenzied as the beasts, for not only was the cattle-boat in some danger, but to appear before Cadwaladr as a fool was one of the worst things that could possibly happen to him. A livid lightning-tree branched towards us from a sudden rent in a blue cloud, to be followed by a clap that seemed to shake the beach and the ribs of the boat. The storm-maddened beast being now beyond control, Jacob was forced to drown his pride before the enemy Bullneck and to cut the animal out of its ropes. It floundered overboard into the sea and staggered up the shingle from which it freed itself in a cloud of flying water and sand, to canter away towards the west side in search of the herd.

21

Cadwaladr was left alone with bitterness on his tongue; for Nans had persuaded her brother to come and spirit away the two younger children.

He was stripped of family in the first autumn days like a tree of leaves. He had no furniture except a table, a couple of chairs, a bed, and an oil stove.

At first, he sought our company; but we found his constant

presence oppressive; he began to tighten his hand over us since he no longer had his family by; I was afraid of staying in the house alone lest he suddenly come in, particularly after one day when I happened to be calling unexpectedly at the Levens's. I tapped the door, and opened it, to find myself looking down the barrel of a shotgun, with Mrs. Levens at the other end. Her mouth was set, and her hand was on the trigger.

She said, 'I thought you were Cadwaladr'; relaxed her hand on the gun, and began to shake. Then she cried out, 'If that man comes near my door, I swear I'll shoot him.'

Now he shunned everyone, but he would not be defeated. He went to sea alone, he slept alone, he ate in solitary dignity. His was a kind of heroic madness; and his vanity was so great that he would not admit to being in any way vanquished.

Over on the east side, on the non-human face of the island, seals could be heard roaring loudly as lions at feeding time. The bulls fought, tearing at one another's necks and shoulders.

Rolling through beds of oarweed, a black bull circled a cow who lay, a bloated fat slug, on a tide-left rock. She alternately dozed, her head falling towards the waves; then jerked upright, staring with patient eyes. When the bull tried to mount beside her she snarled and snapped at him.

Up on the land, down in the sea, the fight for existence never slackened. While Cadwaladr menaced the world with the limb of a tree, two bull seals, a young pretender and an old king would be roaring and battling among the kelp, making more cheerless the desolate water-meadows.

Cadwaladr's dog reflected the nature of his master. Just as Stewart's lean hound had shown something of the thin disconsolate man in his character, so did Cadwaladr's old bitch give a clue to her master's nature. Deaf and blind, quartering her small world, secretive and distrustful, she recognised no man as friend. Set obstinately on a course, she was sensitive to anyone approaching; she side-tracked the person in her path, disappearing through a hole in the hedge until they had passed, when she would emerge: lift a blind face, nostrils twitching, to get the scent of him who had gone by. She moved in an aura of fear, which she had shared with the children and with Nans.

22

We had one final happiness with the children before they were taken away. We picnicked with them and Cadwaladr on Craig y Llanw. It was a fine Sunday and a very low tide.

Cadwaladr and Paul carried our boat across the narrow neck of land between the Cafn and Porth Clegyr, and from there we passed over to the islet, dragging the boat up on to the skerry before exploring the deep gutters and crabholes. Tudur and his father ran from hole to hole, bringing out mammoth crabs such as I had never seen before.

Siani, who was ordinarily sullen and unfriendly, was on this day radiant. In the corner of the clothes chest she had found a fragment of coarse lace which after the addition of a blue ribbon, she had converted into a sun-bonnet.

Craig y Llanw stands only a few feet above the waves even at low water. On the west, facing towards South America, it shelves so gradually that one feels it should be possible to wade far out into the ocean, towards the shipping lanes.

This was the extreme western edge of our world. The children were on the border of their world too, but in another sense, for, in a few weeks' time, the sound of surf creaming on the inlet, the taste of cold coffee, the flavour of lemonade drunk with the tide running through the bottom of the bottle, the clean smell of their father's white shirt, his unexpected mood of gaiety, would be forgotten under the impact of new and disturbing impressions from the outside world.

23

At certain times of the year, a phenomenally high tide visits this shore. As it falls towards full ebb, a sandy plain is left for the wonderment of the few inhabitants of the island. It is level, shining sand, compact and dry. Here and there on the immense tract, a solitary object is left; a convoluted whelk or fanshell; sometimes, a red stone of jasper veined with white, curiously polished and shaped by sea-action, may be picked up by a beach-combing child.

At this period, the fishermen put upright poles into the sand, tie cross-pieces to them, and on to these primitive structures hang out their brown nets to dry. They form on the lonely new beach intimate areas behind which the children delight to play. These young children are of dark Iberian stock. Through the action of winds, their black hair stands out stiffly, as if some kind of seaweed covered their heads. Their faces have already the closed unexpectant look of their elders, for they know none of the small intimate delights and surprises of childhood that are commonplace in more civilised and mother-protected regions of the earth.

They are stocky and small for their age. Through centuries of in-breeding, they have faces of the same pattern; tending to heaviness of bone; the skin thick and weathered to a dusky brick-bronze; the short nose rather flat, the eyes large and of a surprisingly clear grey under knitted black brows that meet over the bridge of the nose; the mouth full and sensuous. Arms and legs show an unusual muscular power. The children have been bowlegged since infancy through carrying nets and boat tackle and sacks of meal. Though they show deformation, the legs of these children are rounded and firm-fleshed, with the texture of grained egg-shell.

They walk then, on this day after the night of extremely high water, down on to the clean sand; five children, three boys and two girls. It is a calm day. On the newly exposed beach no wind walks, but the air is full of the distant menace of surf breaking on the long shore. The children play among the herring-net screens.

One has found a coloured ball in the sea, which he rolls slowly under the sole of his naked foot. The other boys have wooden hoops. The youngest girl hovers about her brothers.

The other girl, who wears a striped dress, has found a sea-gull with a broken wing. She nurses the dying bird. Far away, the fifth child, more adventurous than the rest, bowls his hoop at the tide-edge.

24

On August the fifteenth (the Vigil of our Lady's Assumption) Cadwaladr, while digging in his garden, disinterred the bones of a saint; then he came upon many skeletons; skulls and thigh bones, teeth all brown like pre-Columbian pottery; shards that crumbled at the touch of spade and fingers, even as the air flowed over them . . .

By evening, we had grown disgusted with ourselves for having handled the skeletons, for it was clear, the warning on the saints' cross in the churchyard:

'Respect the remains of 20,000 saints buried nearby: in hoc loco requiescant in pace.'

'Safe in this island where each saint wished to be buried near the sound of the ever-changing tides.'

Feverishly, we washed and washed our hands, to deny having touched the bones.

This event put me in mind of my momentary 'vision' in the summer. On the Sunday of August the thirtieth, the day of St. Rose of Lima: whilst walking along the west side, and happening to look up towards Pant and the ruins on the hill, I had seen the living abbey; its shape and extent, its hive-activity; the smoke of its kitchens, the keen industry of its fertile gardens; its physical labour, prayer and contemplation; monks reading the Office for the day, or sitting relaxed at open windows, with their sandalled feet thrust out into the sunlight.

25

Behind the task of running a household, and of being part of a community with all it entailed of co-operative action with regard to boats and cattle and sheep, I managed by sheer stubbornness, to continue my real life, which is of the imagination.

This was at all times less than easy, but I gradually adjusted myself to constant and violent changes of occupation: after hauling a boat or herding cows, to turn with minimum strain to painting or writing.

I was in the habit of carrying scraps of paper about with me, on which to put down word-germs, the secret life of poetry.

Becoming obsessed with the making of a poem, I would work at the words, always cutting away; trying to make little express much; condensing, clarifying, and finally forging. Page after page of the notebook would become covered with countless variations of the one poem that might be taken up and laid aside over a period of weeks or months or even years.

The making of a poem is for me an almost endless process; even when at last it sounds to be complete, it seems best to put it away for further ripening and a more dispassionate assessment at a later time.

. . . Blessed Rose . . . nourished betimes with the dew of thy grace, should blossom in the far Indies . . . the fragrance of her passage beckons us . . . to become a perfume offered . . .*

I

> Rose of Lima! Rose of Lima!
> The fragrance of your passing
> Stirs me to remember the island
> Remembers me of the island
> Which like a bride wears proudly
> A jewel at the breast's hollow
> Of pigeon-curving bone, perfumed
> With cassia, myrrh, and aloe

*from the Missal: Masses of the Saints.

A barbar-coloured, wave-worn pebble
Burnt with sea-light; clasp, exotic Rose

                                  dark
Warm rock for the palm, in your damp cell!
                                  dank

2

Rose of Lima! Rose of Lima!
The fragrance of your passing
Summons me to the island

Which like a bride does not forget
The jewel at the breast's hollow

The decorated bone perfumed
With cassia myrrh and aloe

This barbar-coloured wave-worn pebble
Burnt with sea-light; clasp, exotic Rose

A stone for the palm, in your dark cell!

3

Rose of Lima! Rose of Lima!

The fragrance of your passing
Reminds me of the island
Which like a bride wears proudly
Perfumed with cassia myrrh and aloe
A jewel at the breast's hollow
Of pigeon-curving bone

This barbar-coloured, wave-worn pebble
Burnt with sea-light; clasp, exotic Rose

Warm rock for the palm, in your dark cell!

183

26

The house threatened under the blows and torrents of our first winter to fall down over our heads; already, there was a gaping hole in the roof, but we had to be patient for some time yet, until the Levens's were ready to make the move up to Garthwen. When at last they had taken their belongings out of Pen Craig, it was simplicity itself to load our furniture on to the pony cart and to take it down to our new house. Just in time! The week after we vacated the old house, the last remaining good bedroom became uninhabitable when in a severe gale the big skylight blew out of the roof to shatter in fragments on the cobbles below.

Paul had already decided to go into a sort of uneasy partnership with Bill Levens: to share the grazing of the middle of the island. So we bought a cow due to have her first calf. She was a fine Welsh Black of uncertain temperament, full of a devilish spite and egotism.

We named her Sophia, and her calf, Marie: she proved to be a wonderful milker.

In that same autumn of 1948; on a dark night, Jacob knocked at the door in a state of suppressed excitement. He had been over to the mainland.

'Bring out a lamp and look at what I have got for you,' he said. In a wheel-barrow, curled up in a sack, was a strong black bull-calf. His head was square, and between his nubbly rudimentary horns was a mass of gleaming curls. He had big mild eyes with long eye-lashes.

He was christened José, and handed over to me for rearing. Of the many animals I have reared the little black bull was the most tractable and rewarding. He ate his gruel steadily, without greed or waste; and his gentleness was a wonder to see. Everyone told us:

'Ah, a black bull, that one will be dangerous. They always are.'

But he was not. Sometimes, in his youth, when his horns were growing fast, he would roar and playfully dig his head into an earth bank, so that he would become covered with a powdering of soil; but with us he was utterly to be trusted. Sophie vented the full force of her malice upon him while he was still a calf; particularly when the herd was being driven back to the yard at night in winter-time. She would harry the bull-calf until she had him sprawled on his back unable to move from the thickset hedge. We knew what she in her arrogance did not know, that one day José would be a full-grown bull ready to get his revenge. One evening, a year or so later, Sophia came in for milking with one horn hanging by a thread. José had won his first battle with her.

Around Christmas-time of 1948 a fat goose escaped from the mainland, alighted on the island, and was at once pursued by Cadwaladr and Paul. Clutching their guns, the two enemies spent several days on their stomachs within a few yards of one another, in the stinking bed of seaweed that the gales had formed in Porth Clegyr where the goose was now living. It was a wary bird; when it sensed the man's presence, it took to the surf. It seemed not improbable that the goose would eventually find itself in a position between the two armed men, and that they would lose their heads and wing one another instead of the bird. After three or four days of patient manoeuvres, Paul returned triumphant with the dead goose.

'It will make a wonderful present for my parents,' I said, as we plucked it; hoping there would be a quiet day on which to send gifts to our families and friends ashore.

More days passed.

As we ate the goose, we sighed with melancholy contentment.

'What a shame! The parents would have liked this bird. It has a fine flavour.'

By 1950, Marie was also in milk, which meant we could rear calves, have plenty of milk for the house, and make Cornish cream and a little butter, since we had now two good yielders. We had in addition to cattle, a bacon pig named Humff, a flock of geese, a few elderly ducks, and a yard-full of hens.

Of the bullocks we reared, one was a little mad, and would race up and down the fields in fruitless quests. When at last in his maturity he was sold and taken over to the mainland, no sooner had he touched the shore than he swam out to sea. Fortunately, there was a man fishing in the cove, who was able to get a rope round his horns and to tow him back to land.

By this year 1950, we had a herd of eight cattle, including the bull who was now used for general service to all the island cows with the exception of those belonging to Cadwaladr. Since the 'Battle on the mountain' he had been outlawed from all communal activity. In addition to the cattle, we had fifty-six head of sheep; by 1951, we had eighty-six head. In 1952, we tried the experiment of wintering six cross-Highland bullocks from a friend's herd. In the winter of 1953, we had six Highland heifers; and our sheep count was up to one hundred and twenty-six.

27

It seemed as if there would be no end to the horror of this disastrous winter.

A few days before Christmas, a child died. Somewhere in the world an infant dies every hour; but not within living memory had a baby died here; so its death was more than usually calamitous.

Dic Longshanks and his wife had already four children; the eldest not yet five years old when the fifth was born. No sooner had one been born than the next had been conceived. It was a hard life for

Leah, being tied to a primitive farmhouse, with babies tumbling about her feet wherever she moved. She had no escape, no relaxation. Dic, being of a roving, unstable disposition, liked the freedom of the place, for here he was his own master; whereas on the mainland, he would have been a farm servant or a road-mender.

A sign that disaster was coming to the farm Clogwyn had been given the previous summer, leaving the mark of ill-omen on the house. A few days after it had been stacked, Dic had had the misfortune to lose his hay by fire; the rick bursting into flame without apparent cause.

Dic and the other men were out on the sea lifting their lobster pots when the hay began to smoulder.

Leah, who was seven months heavy with child, on going out at the back door to fetch water from the well, saw a red tongue lick out from the side of the stack. She shut the children in the house, and hurried to Ty Draw, to get help from her sister.

It was some time before the men saw the cloud of smoke rising from the middle of the island. They were just in time to save a little of the hay by dousing the flames with buckets of water carried from the well in the mountain.

Dic's eyes had a haunted look in them after the fire had been put out. We stood resting, our hands and faces streaked with dirt, beside the stinking wreck of the haystack. He must have been thinking as most of us were of an old saying. It was Cadwaladr who put the thoughts into words as those of us who lived in the north were walking home.

'If hay goes on fire at ebb tide, it will bring bad luck to the farmer. If it burns at the flood, it will bring the man good luck.'

The hay had gone on fire as the tide was falling.

Months after, one breakfast time on a morning in late December, Dic came round to tell us that his youngest baby (the one Leah had been carrying inside her at the time of the fire) had died in the blackness before dawn.

This was on a Friday, after a night of storm with fierce gusts from the east leaping the mountain top to batter the houses. Scarcely any of us had slept peacefully that night. Doors had burst open and buckets had flown over the ground. The baby had been sickly for a fortnight, but not ill enough to make his parents uneasy.

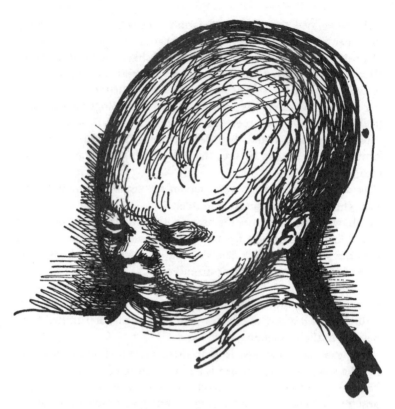

Dic and Leah had sat with the baby by the kitchen fire, not understanding that it was about to die. The breath left it a little after six
o'clock in the morning. The body weighed less at death than at
birth; the limbs were quite shrunken, no bigger than a doll's, and the
face was blue and green and sharp as a bird's.

When it grew light, the father came round the island with the
news. It was too late to fetch a doctor, and the heavy seas made it
impossible for one of our small boats to cross for the coroner. Dic
went up to the lighthouse and had a message sent over the radio
telegraph to the coastguard forty miles away. The coastguard then
telephoned the message to our nearest mainland village with the news.

The sea was hungry; the noise of it had hurt our ears for days.
Huge foam-crested waves broke on one another's backs in their
haste to pass our shores.

On Saturday afternoon, permission was received by wireless for the child to be buried without an inquest. After the message came, three amateur grave-diggers went by on the path, through the incessant grey downpouring of rain. The men were tall and black in rain-sodden oilskins and sea boots. Each man carried a spade over his shoulder. They were Dic, his brother-in-law Jacob, and the sea-wrinkled Cadwaladr.

There was a pale exhausted light in the sky after days and nights of storm. A heavy swell was breaking against the black cliffs. The men spent the afternoon in the graveyard, digging a deep hole. Meanwhile, Bill Levens was making a coffin out of driftwood. When the box was finished, he darkened it with floor stain, and fitted a leather strap handle at either end. On the lid he screwed small pieces of copper in the form of a cross.

Soon after dark on Sunday, the evening before the funeral, Bill Levens and his wife and one or two others went to Dic's, to take away the body.

'Where have you put the corpse?' asked Mrs. Levens. Leah went to the dresser, the middle drawer of which was locked. Turning a key in it, she opened the drawer, saying:

'There was nowhere else to put it, to have it out of the hands of the children. They kept wanting to play with it.'

The Levens's fought their way back through driving rain and darkness to the chapel that had not been used for five or six years. After they had arranged the corpse in the fragile coffin, they placed it beside the altar for the night.

We buried the child next day. Soon after breakfast, I saw Dic passing up the lane. A little later, he returned carrying in his hand a pair of shining Sunday boots. He had borrowed a suit and boots from Owain in order to appear respectable at the funeral, for he had nothing of his own to wear except his ragged fishing clothes.

Around eleven o'clock, two lightkeepers joined the chief islander at the door of his workshop; after them, came the bereaved parents. They were followed by Jacob and Eira.

In the sun and wind that made of the water green and purple meadows, a wine-dark Odyssean sea, eleven of us gathered in the chapel.

The children had been left at home in charge of Rhiannon. We scarcely knew one another in our best clothes. The patriarchal figure in the wide-brimmed black hat, looking like a preacher, was Cadwaladr.

My God, Cadwaladr in mourning!

Black tie, white collar, a dark suit, and a hat like a sombrero.

Feet shuffled on the tiled floor of the mildew-smelling chapel. The service, which only lasted a few minutes, was conducted by the Ancient Mariner, who read a few short prayers, hurrying over them, for he was unnerved by the terrible sobbing of the mother. We did not sing; it being winter, there were no flowers. We could not trust ourselves to sing; and there were no flowers in December.

We filed out into the weak sunlight, past the ruined tower of the abbey to the grave that was already half-full of clay-coloured water. The doll-coffin was lowered on a thick white cord. In the west corner of the graveyard, an effigy of an angel stood in solitude, holding out her arms to the whirlpools and twisting currents below. She was marble, and a prisoner in a whitewashed wire cage.

Poor angel! I had several times tried to force the padlock chaining the gate to an iron upright at one of the corners. I had never succeeded in opening it, and had always had to walk away, pretending a detachment; walking carefully between the sarcophagi and the drunken headstones; saying to myself:

'She is only a marble effigy, and they have put a wire net over the creature so the gulls may not soil her garments and wings.'

But that was a terrible thought. Not even the birds might touch her. There were always refinements to horror; one day, a wren had found its way through the mesh and was beating itself to death in attempts to get out again.

'Here lies the child Ianto who will never sail the summer seas, nor with his father fish for fine lobster, nor know the dangers of winter in the Sound.'

28

Though she was made of harder, more durable stuff than Alice Hopkinson, Mrs. Levens was equally dissatisfied with island life. She had struggled now for what seemed to her to be a reasonable time

to make the venture a success; it failed to show signs of succeeding.

She could never overcome her fear of animals. If no one else was about, she called upon me to bring in her cows, to help herd her sheep. She was a sort of female overseer, full of spite and energy. She never hesitated; but would burst into the house, demanding that Paul should come at once to do her bidding. She hated to be mistaken for an islander, which meant she was always unsuitably clad for such a rough place. In winter-time, she unbent sufficiently to smoke a clay pipe beside the hearth. Her husband who was an inveterate smoker, when tobacco failed, would smoke anything he could lay hands on: dried parsley, burdock leaves, even on one occasion, silage from Cadwaladr's stack.

Bill Levens believed in an easy life of minimum effort. He hated to hurry; he was a born potterer, and most of his time was spent in his workshop where he played with the motors of ancient outboard engines, or made ships and doll-houses for his children. He wanted the island, but he had no patience for animals, and had nothing to say to lobster-fishing.

Alongside two derelict island craft lay the Levens's iron boat. Bill had worked on her for years; as fast as he scraped and painted her, the rust worked, wearing her plates thin. She was not launched until the day she was towed away to be sold for scrap metal.

At the end of three years therefore, the inevitable happened;

he was forced to go back ashore and take up his old job or become insolvent.

Within a week of coming to their decision, the Levenses left; and the Dic Longshanks family too; for Leah had never got over the death of her child. Life here had always been impossible for her, with no chance of ever getting away from the children for an hour's peace. Now, having been found by Dici one night trying to hold her head underwater in the well in the mountain, the man was at last forced to take her and the children off the island.

29

The Levenses had a savage boar running with their sows. Out of sheer perversity, he had been christened Violet. He, Violet, was the terror of the middle fields, for he had an ugly temper and could move as fast as a dog. A grunt mixed with a squeal, a flap of bristling ear, and Violet was upon you. He had been a placid pig in early youth when a goat belonging to the Ancient Mariner fell in love with him. Every afternoon, they took a siesta together under the studio window. The young pig was never allowed to change his position: the goat pinned him firmly with a foreleg. By the end of July he had become so blistered with sunburn about the ears and body that for the rest of the hot weather he had to be kept in a sty.

The day arrived for the departure of the Levens family and whippet and cats and boar. Shouting directions from a safe distance, Mrs. Levens superintended his progress to the sea. Violet was determined not to leave the island without a battle. The more we tried to push his sullen bulk down the shingle, the more settled became his stance. His mistress grew hysterical, torn between the necessity of getting him aboard the cattle boat, and horror of our treatment of her valuable beast.

All things pass: a chastened Violet was eventually netted in the boat, and peace fell with the departure of the family. Without a backward glance, without a thank you for the help we had given, they went out of our lives.

By some means, we did hear an item of news concerning the fate of Violet. He was so upset at being torn out of his island context that immediately on reaching his destination in the south of England, he attacked and badly tore up a man's arm: and had to be shot.

Alas, lice-infested Violet, first and last of boars.

30

'The boat is going over.' That phrase had an electrifying importance for us, always; for it meant mail and food and news from the outer world. The men would shave and wash and change their clothes in a frenzy of impatience, while the women made out the shopping lists, carefully checking up on the sacks and tins of emergency stores.

At the two hours' ebb, we would stand at the water's edge laughing, because our bodies were glowing from the exercise of pushing down the boats from the grass above the shore; and we would shade our eyes so that we could see more clearly our men in the boat. The ritual was always the same.

In the moments before the boat went, I would think, 'Did I order flour? Have we enough salt for curing the pig?'

'When will you be back?'

'Between four and five,' or whatever the time might be, dictated by the state of the tide. Boats left the island for the mainland at two hours' ebb, and returned to the island just after low water.

The engine would be opened out to full throttle; the tow-rope would tauten between the two boats: they were away.

There was Twm, the owner of the boat; his brother-in-law of the insolent never-to-be-trusted smile; next to him in the bows would be my husband in a red woollen cap; and next to him the Ancient Mariner dreaming of an idle day ashore.

Lying back in the dinghy and already more than half asleep, would be Bill Levens, his arm thrown negligently over the tiller.

31

In winter-time we were sometimes cut off for as long as three weeks by heavy seas. One household would lend a candle here, borrow a gallon of paraffin there, do a little careful bartering. The men haunted the coves for driftwood. At such times, scarcely a trail of

smoke went up from our chimneys. A sack of flour would last a long time, but fresh yeast soon lost its virtue, and tinned dried yeast was relatively difficult to obtain. Potatoes, having to be shared out between humans and pigs, would be eaten all too soon; of carrots and turnips we had usually a sufficiency, stored in sand.

There was always enough to eat, but the monotonous diet became suffocating. Every day we ate rabbit: fried, boiled, roasted, or made into patés French style. Rabbit never palled. In a place where fish, game, shellfish, home-baked bread, and fresh vegetables were eaten, tinned food had no savour and was only eaten in emergencies.

32

If it was a peaceful day, and it could be peaceful and bland even in November, it was possible to do without a fire and to have the windows open all day in the dining-room that faced the south west. Only the flocks of geese, white clusters on the still green land, restlessly cried and flapped their wings, disturbing the silence.

Intensely quiet periods alternating with pounding seas and melancholy winds, unnerved newcomers to island life.

The men were over to the mainland; the farms were asleep, apart from the sporadic crowing of cocks and the quarrelling of geese. The air was laced with shining cobwebs.

33

As the sun went down, I walked over the mountain to Jacob's farm, and helped his wife and daughter to get in the calves and milking cows, and to feed the bony white mare after his work at the treadmill churn. Afterwards, we climbed to the lookout hut. Sitting on the rock-shelf, in the bitter cold of evening with the cliffs falling sheer from our feet, we stared out over the cold Sound for signs of a boat.

Rhiannon cried out after we had been there for some time:

'There she is; just off the point.'

For a second or two, a pinpoint had been visible as it rounded the headland. After that, it was again invisible, for it was keeping well in under the cliffs of the mainland before coming out into the Race.

By the time we reached the boathouse, it was already dark. To the south, an enormous cloud in the shape of a man toppled over the lighthouse that was weaving its beam across the dulling water and the cold earth.

Crouched against a buttress of the wall to get some shelter from the piercing wind, the woman beside me watched the flashes of the lantern. Though only a foot away from me physically, she was a lifetime away in thought. Her mouth was set; her whole face concentrated on recapturing an overpowering emotion from the past. Beautiful, stern, enigmatic woman.

Eira crouched near her, in lee of the other supporting wall, but in how different an attitude. She was relaxed and peaceful with in-experience while her mother was tense with inward rebelliousness bred from dislike of the island and bitter memories.

A dark mass became detached from the rocky entrance to the anchorage, to float out onto the water. Here they come, the three small boats strung out, the men standing motionless in the first boat. Are all safe, are they all there, our men? One, two, three, four, five, all are safe.

But three strange figures were huddled in the second boat. Lighting a hurricane lamp, we slithered across the naked rock to the beach.

Silently, carrying the sacks and boxes of provisions, we passed one another on the slippery seaweed. It smelt like long-rotten cabbages. Then began the procession to the boathouse.

The three figures were standing together, as if they feared us; as I passed by, I peered into the face of a woman. It was Nans; and with her were Tudur and Siani.

34

So, only a few months after she had 'Gone away for ever' Nans had returned with the two youngest children; eager as a girl in her first love-affair, with wild tales of her dear Cadwaladr, her darling man.
· With this reversal of emotion we could not cope; having been so

closely embroiled once in the Bullnecks' domestic troubles, we were more than a little shy of being fooled again.

Death had now taken up residence in Nans's face: but as for Tudur, we could scarcely bear to look at him, for he being more sensitive than the rest of his family, shook continuously as if from ague; no doubt from the shock of having been brought back to so much savagery and hatred, just as he was beginning to grow accustomed to a more gentle life.

35

From each new and thrilling experience the life of the imagination is reborn giving the illusion that here at last is a true flowering; the beginning from which great things will come; either through love, or through the making of a poem, a painting or a piece of music. From the encountered person or object, a power of creative energy streams out.

The imagination has been pricked forward many times. Perhaps this is the last romance of my life; a thing of shadows and seafog, a memory of rain.

It is only in voluntary imprisonment that I can bring out the painful fruits of experience. Having spent most of my days too close to nature, I have had time to discover that nature is not enough. The island has succeeded in making me love mankind; crowded Piccadilly, quaysides, foreign cities, exotic fruits, faces, gatherings, le Corbusier's architecture.

Away with the nature lover. For the nature fancier is the town dweller with a sentimental view of wild things.

My fellow islanders (Nature's children, realistic souls) are almost without exception bitten by the lust for gold. To give an example: Jacob. He wets a finger to test the wind; and a pound note sticks to it.

36

For a long time, almost a year on and off, I was obsessed with the idea of a woman's archaic bronze head having been found by chance

and raised from the seabed to strong southern light; theme, I
suppose of death into life, darkness overcome by dayspring; the
unity of our universe; under-water and earthly; the sponge-fisher
and the goddess, the intact though shipwrecked woman's face,
Aegean tears still wet upon her cheeks.

I

Recovered from deep water (about) a mile from shore
   the sea off Asia Minor
Bust of the age of Praxiteles
Veiled, with bowed head, mourning mother goddess
Demeter, by Turkish sponge fishers
The metal thickly encrusted, except for the face
Which is unharmed. It was lying in the sand of the seabed
(Or de-ess of an unknown cult
the soft pillow of the seabed had not harmed)

Shipwrecked Demeter,
if it is indeed she,
A new Demeter
Gold-incrusted, bronze-breasted;
Shipwrecked, veiled, intact of face;
Demeter the mourning mother,
(If it is she or another
unknown goddess) raised by Turkish
sponge fishers off Asia Minor;
Has conserved force from the seabed
Where the dark centuries held her,
And with salt-burned gaze
Gives, under an older sun, solace
For nerve-shaken times.

A new Demeter
From the August wave, a mile from shore,
Turkish sponge fishers raised the new Demeter
Shipwrecked, veiled, intact of face
The mourning-mother Demeter
(If it is she) or an unknown goddess
Has been raised by sponge fishers
From the August-green (wave) water
Off Asia Minor

Shipwrecked, veiled, intact of face:
The mourning-mother Demeter,
If it is she; or an unknown goddess;
Has been raised by a sponge fisher
From August-green water
Off Asia Minor

Shipwrecked Demeter	The new Demeter if it is indeed Demeter
Raised from the wave (midsummer wave)	Recovered from deep water a mile from shore
Lying face downward in the sand of the seabed	The gaze of the mourning mother
Veiled	Features intact in the sand
Bronze breast with green and gold incrustation	
An older sun now burns her lights	her morning face mourning-mother
face (mother-mourning face)	
The new Demeter If it is you she	a shipwrecked goddess

If indeed you are the shipwrecked goddess

Recovered from the August wave, a mile from shore
Raised by Turkish sponge fishers raised you
Intact from the seabed sand
Where she had lain face downward
Conserving force for our nerve-shaken day
Veiled, bronze-breasted,
Crusted with green and gold/green and gold incrusted/
Recovered intact, a mile from shore
She could be raised intact, a mile from shore

(Gold-ecrusted, bronze-ebrusted
Shipwrecked veiled intact of face)

(Demeter the mourning-mother
O if it is she or another goddess)

(Raised by Turkish sponge fishers
From August-green water off Asia Minor)

(Has conserved strength from the seabed
Where the dark centuries held her)

(And with salt-strengthened gaze
Gives under an older sun solace)

Gold-incrusted, bronze-breasted
Shipwrecked, veiled, intact of face

Demeter, the mourning mother
Raised by Turkish sponge fishers
From August-green water, off Asia Minor

Has conserved force from the seabed
Where the dark centuries held her
Smothered by dark centuries of sand
Intact though shipwrecked

37

Nans was rapidly becoming an invalid; lying upstairs propped with pillows so that she could look into the fields. When it rained she complained that it would never become fine enough for the hay to be saved; but she held her peace when the sun came out to dry the grasses and the withered flowers.

She was a shrivelled monkey, the weight of years of ill-health oppressed her. She used to strike her withered breasts under the corset-bones, and whisper to me:

'It is here. Here it is, the pain. I do not want to live.'

She often took my hand in hers to say:

'Your hand is warm. I am always cold these days.'

38

Alas, good Jesus, Nans has died as she said she would, before she was more than middle-aged.

Tonight, ghosts walk in the farm among the people who whisper round the hearth. She is dead now and ready for her coffin, wet earth, and the maggot of the graveyard.

Not a tear was shed for Nans, not even by the youngest child Siani. In fact Siani and Tudur looked more than usually pleased with life, as they whistled about their tasks on the farm.

I went up into the room where the candle-flame seemed to make the body live; I was afraid of the corpse, small and yellow in the bed. It seemed wrong that no window had been opened to let the spirit out into the darkness; but perhaps her spirit would not be in need of the air and the night-wind, but would be pleased enough at first to move about the house.

Every adult islander was there, solemn in chapel clothes. The men did not speak as they ate; the women murmured together, and drank a little tea.

The yard was quiet. There is a poor dead woman in the house; a poor body that wanted to rest. She had suffered enough for two, and had no more strength left; the juice had dried out of her bones.

I remembered how the geese had flown to mob her when she crossed the yard to the closet, coming at her with proud heads and beating her legs with their wings.

As she had lain dying, they had propped her under the shoulders so that there were pits of sunken flesh behind her collar bones. She had prayed and sung then, saying we must pray and sing with her. One day, as she was praying, a day on which Cadwaladr had gone out fishing alone, Owain came into the room to say that the dealer had unexpectedly come from the mainland to buy some calves.

She stopped saying Our Father and spoke sharply to her son:
'Do not let them go for small money. Make him pay.'
When we were alone again, she gripped my hand and spoke softly:
'We must have money; always money.'
Then changing her tone:
'Thy will be done on earth as it is in heaven.'

39

Cadwaladr who had been unmoved by the illness and ultimate death of his wife, was at last shaken by superstitious fear when, in the evening after the funeral, the ceiling of the Best Room fell down over the place where the coffin had rested between two chairs. He thought it was a judgement, and sat for hours at the kitchen table with his cap covering the tell-tale eyes.

40

Tudur and I had not been together since his mother's death. A few days after the funeral, we met.

I said, 'Tudur, I am so sorry about your mother. It is very bad for you to have lost her like this.'

A radiant grin spread over his face.

'Ay,' he roared. 'Funny; isn't it?'

After a long pause, he roared out again.

'The old ram died last week, too. Funny, isn't it?'

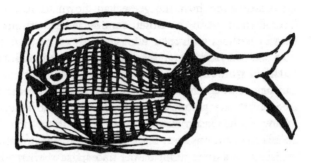

41

There are certain states of frustration that drive one almost beyond endurance, to the borders of insanity.

Thus it must have been with the young Pole who had set himself to become our holy man.

We had had our King; our bad man Caliban Cadwaladr; and for contrast, the clown Merfyn; our Ancient Mariner; our Rose of the wilderness, Eira; even our own hermit.

For three years, the hermit was our nearest neighbour, though we saw little of him. During his last year on the island, he lived in almost total darkness, being shut away during daylight hours behind closely blanketed windows, and only venturing out under cover of night.

Winter and summer, he dressed himself in a thick woollen hat, a ragged fur-collared wind-cheater roped tightly at the waist, thick trousers, and high canvas footwear which he called his Easter boots. He allowed his brown wavy hair to grow shoulder-length; he was bearded, hollow-cheeked, dirty, and unkempt.

He was a Polish immigrant who had landed in Britain after the War; no one knew for what reason. He had suddenly arrived on the island one autumn night and had set up residence in Garthwen which had just been vacated by Stewart and Alice.

At the time of his arrival, he was a personable young man, cleanly dressed and full of gaiety.

His avowed intention was to become a holy man; with prayer and fasting to make his contribution to the fight against Lucifer and his black angels. Somewhere, in this dark experiment conducted alone in his pride and stubbornness, things began to go wrong. He developed a fear of sunlight, even of the air of common day; not God but the Devil answered his call, until the house itself in which he had conjured the spirits to rise, became for him the ultimate in horror.

His shunning of us his neighbours, became so extreme that months went by without our seeing him; the only proof we had of his being alive was the shining of his lamp between the chinks of heavily-curtained windows.

Letters came for him, and he answered them; incoming and outgoing mail was placed in a biscuit-tin outside his gate.

How did he exist through the last week of his three years' stay on the island? Paul was away for a few days; it was just after New Year; the island was quite desolate, the time of year when whole days can go by without one's seeing a neighbour.

We sensed that the man was near his breaking-point; he had gone out one night before the final catastrophe, and visited each house in turn, gabbling excited nonsense like a drunken man, pulling at his clothes, and shouting. In one house he had said he was starving and they gave him food; sugar and flour. In another house, he declared he was ill and they gave him a bottle of tonic. His story to me was this; he was coming out into the world with the New Year just commenced. My offers of food he refused.

We were finding the strain of this man's presence amongst us very great. Our nerves became torn to a quite remarkable degree; we felt the need of a priest. Perhaps for the first time on this island we were terrified in our souls of a fearful darkness that was about to be loosed. We repaired the locks on our doors, and saw to it that our windows could not be opened from the outside.

This fear common to the community was quite different in kind from the terror Cadwaladr had for us in his wild rages; this was the imbalance of a soul.

The last phase began in the early morning of a grim January day; the island boat had gone to the mainland at first light. I walked back from the Cafn with Eira, who was coming to milk the cows for me while Paul was away.

A few minutes after I had entered the house, Eira came running in distress. She was still carrying the empty milking pail, and her face was white and terrified.

'Can you hear Wolfgang?' she cried. 'He is yelling and cursing! Can't you hear him?'

I had heard; I could hear, nothing.

We went out on to the bank of the upper field; the most terrible shrieks and ravings were coming from Garthwen; full-throated, they seemed like imprecations, or words garbled at random from the Mass. Wolfgang was either in mortal combat with the Devil or he was murdering someone. We remembered how Rhiannon had told us she would be going up at that time to Garthwen to let out the cattle; it was possible the madman had sprung upon her unawares while she was littering the beasts there.

By ill-chance, there was no man nearer than in the lighthouse. It seemed too dangerous an act to pass Garthwen on the road; but we had to make sure that Rhiannon was safe. Therefore, we took to the fields, forcing our way through the hedges and swamps below Garthwen. There was no sign of human life; the shouting had stopped, but the cart-horses were standing at the field's edge near the corner of the north wall of the house, transfixed with raised heads as if they heard yet the echoes of dreadful cries.

Wolfgang had been in mortal combat with devils. The devil has got him.

Rhiannon was safely at home, and unaware of any catastrophe. Owing to the wind being in the south east, she had heard nothing from up the island.

I left them together, and ran to the lighthouse, to beg that a message be sent to the mainland, asking Jacob to bring back a doctor and a priest; and that men from the lighthouse should go to Garthwen to find out what had happened to the unhappy Pole.

Two of the men there, laughed tolerantly, spoke of 'women' contemptuously, and refused to send a message. To my surprise, Merfyn alone did not mock. After all, he had lived in the shadows with ghosts and strange beings the whole of his life, so that this was to him an inevitable part of existence. He, quite calmly, went alone to Garthwen, where he had to break open the door. It was some time before he could find Wolfgang. The young man was cowering in a dark, barricaded room, and was holding a crowbar ready to attack. The madman collapsed when confronted by the lighthouse-keeper, and was difficult to raise up from the floor.

The room was in the greatest disorder; the standard lamp had been smashed; the radio too; the wallpaper had been torn in shreds from the walls.

Wolfgang, when he could speak, for the paroxysms of passion had exhausted him, said he had been praying the whole night through because it had been his birthday. He had not eaten anything for several days, and there were no signs of food in the house. He had been in the habit of boiling cabbage stalks and drinking the liquid. Cigarette ash and hundreds of cigarette ends littered the floor.

Merfyn took food to him; then he came to me for matches with which to light Wolfgang's stove; and I sent up a bowl of soup.

From the morning of the fifth until shortly before dawn on the next day, we lived in nightmare. Now we knew; the man was mad, shut away in his own hell at Garthwen. This was the bitter realism of the end, for the man who had set out to be our Saint John the Baptist.

Poor tortured, damned soul. Hearing his cries, we had realised the unutterable anguish of his spiritual chaos.

Now, for some hours there was a silence while we waited for him to recoup his strength and break out again.

What were we to do? Merfyn said the crisis had now passed and that Wolfgang was rational again though exhausted by the paroxysms and stresses he had endured throughout the previous night.

Towards dusk, he set out again, running to the lighthouse to demand that his hair and beard should be cut as 'he might be going away for a long time'; then he went to Jacob's where Eira and Rhiannon had fits of hysteria, so great was their fear of him. He told Jacob he was about to die; his time was upon him.

He fell forward on the ground near the churnhouse, and began a wild prayer.

Jacob persuaded him to go back to Garthwen, accompanying him as far as the gate; and was on his way home again, when he heard Wolfgang panting behind him, in mortal dread of being left alone.

It had come to him at last, after the months and years of cutting himself off from mankind and turning only to God (his own version of God) that without the help of man he could not hope to find God. He needed us; at the thirteenth hour, how greatly he needed us.

Seized by panic, he rushed again to the lighthouse and was taken back home in the early dark by Merfyn: Wolfgang was now in terror of the house that for so long had been his only sanctuary against the powers of darkness. Merfyn came to see me after this, bringing back the bowl in which I had sent the soup in the morning. We were sitting talking quietly and sadly of Wolfgang, before the fire, when the terrible bellowing began. This was Bashan's bull, in truth.

'Merfyn! Merfyn! Merfyn!' The voice screamed for its sheet-anchor, the quaking, shrinking Merfyn. Before we had time to do anything, Wolfgang was screaming at the window; then he fell to beating on the door. The flimsy lock gave way, and the maniac was in the doorway. Throwing himself so violently upon Merfyn that he was thrust back into the room, he cried hoarsely, 'Save me! Save me! Paul is after me. He is outside the door, poor devil.'

We tried to quieten him, saying that Paul was away, not on the island at all; but he was beyond comprehension, and whispered to me, 'Hide me in the most secret cupboard; in the dark; anywhere; under the stairs, away from the devils.'

He struggled to open the door to the chamber where wood was stored.

We coaxed him forward into the warmth of the kitchen, but he could not bear the brightness of the lamp, and muttered:

'The light, the light. It is too bright. Put it out.' Turning to me and gripping me tightly, he moaned hoarsely:

'Give me a gun; give me a gun.'

Struggling to maintain a pretence of quietness, I said:

'And what would you be wanting with a gun?'

Outside, the darkness was complete; there was half a gale blowing. We had no means of communication with our neighbours to warn them, or to ask their assistance in our predicament.

We persuaded Wolfgang to sit before the fire, with his back to the lamp. He looked like an old man; his knees buckling under him. He shook uncontrollably, and was constantly on the verge of hysteria. I knew that Paul had some cheroots in the dresser drawer, left over from Christmas; I gave one of them to the Pole, and he alternately sucked at the cheroot and gulped at a cup of coffee.

Once, happening to touch his left arm in order to draw his attention to what I was saying, he startled me by snarling like a tiger. He was, in these last hours sometimes cunning, sometimes animal in his ferocity; at other times, pathetic as a child. When the shaking fits became unbearably severe, Merfyn would lean forward and grip the madman's knee convulsively, saying:

'Now, now; we are your friends. We'll let nothing bad happen to you.'

Shivering, he muttered, 'You don't know what I have seen . . . such things. I cannot tell you; I'll tell you some other time.' This was accompanied by such a dreadful look that I could almost visualise the fiends of his imagination.

Suddenly, hysteria overcame him and he fell forward on to the hearthstone, breaking out into a terrible travesty of the Mass. This was too much; I went into the dairy to get away from the insane babbling.

'Libera nos, quaesumus, Domine, ab omnibus malis, praeteritis, praesentibus, et futuris—Ne perdas cum impiis, Deus, animam meam, et cum sanguinam vitam meam—'

He was dragged to his feet by Merfyn: he looked round at us dazedly, and stumbling towards the table, made an attempt to bring his arm down on the glass shade of the lamp. There was just time to cry, 'Take care of the lamp!'

Merfyn had him firmly by the arm; I signalled behind Wolfgang's back, that Merfyn should take him to the lighthouse; it was clear now that official action must be taken before there was tragedy.

On the dark, wet, crazy journey to the lighthouse, Wolfgang attempted many times to run away from Merfyn and Jacob, but at last they were in the safety of the lighthouse kitchen. A vigil began; the men taking it in turns to attend to the light in the tower, while the rest held Wolfgang down. He succeeded in breaking one lamp, but was unsuccessful in his efforts to jump through the window. The relief ship had by now been sent for, and she was in constant radio communication with the lighthouse.

Jacob had turned the iron key in the lock on us in Ty Draw. We lay fully clothed on the beds, with lamps burning, listening to the dogs howling on their chains in the yard; to the roaring of the swell on the west side; imagining stealthy footsteps outside the window, listening to the beating of our hearts. We talked at random, to keep fear at bay.

Nobody slept that night.

At two o'clock in the morning, an aeroplane came over, circled the lighthouse and went off again northwards, reassured by the beam still flashing from the tower.

Over the radio telegraph a voice said, 'Now we are approaching the north headland; we have to stand out to sea a little; a strong swell is breaking on the rocks. Now, we are past the peninsula; we are in the Sound; a strong ebb tide is running through with much grumbling of water. We can see the island only dimly; and we are not far enough south yet to see the lighthouse beam.'

(On the ship, over the radio, they could hear the madman's cries.)

And so it went on, until she anchored in the safety of the bay and put down her tender, with two young policemen on board.

At 3.30 in the morning of the seventh of January, Wolfgang, bellowing and raving, hand-cuffed; in a strait-jacket fixed to a stretcher, was removed from the island and taken ashore to the nearest market town, before being sent to a mental hospital.

Jacob told us afterwards at breakfast that never before had he seen such a phenomenon; one whole side of Wolfgang's body was given over to the Devil, the other side to God. One side of his face was evil and twitching; the other side was smooth and placid. His legs shook convulsively; his hands were swollen; his eyes deeply sunken. He had stroked himself on the 'God side'; attacked anyone who approached the 'Devil side'. He had cried out many times, 'Kill and twist; kill and twist' and once, had bitten at Merfyn's arm.

In the last minutes, when he realised that he was being torn out of his dark sanctuary, he became filled with a mortal dread of being taken away; shrieking that he was God, and daring any man to lay hands on him 'who made the moon and the stars.'

I shall never forget the madness of his eyes; or the terrible animal sounds that burst from him, sounds that made him seem both bull and tiger. And yet, at times he was like a small child begging to be comforted.

I thought back over certain remarks he had made, things he had done, which seemed to have a bearing on his gradually worsening mental condition.

On the first Christmas Eve, he had become excessively morbid, seeming to gloat over the marks of the crucifixion on the body of our Lord, examining the palms and wrists of his own hands minutely.

He had spoken of the Day of Judgement; of how the limbs hacked off in wars would rejoin their bodies. He had taken photographs of arms and legs from periodicals, and pasted them in macabre fashion round the bottom of a reproduction of Dali's painting of the crucifixion.

In those early days, while he was still comparatively normal, he asked whether he might visit us sometimes, for it was not an easy thing for him to do; to cut himself off from wine, women, and song.

The summer before, he had told me:

'I don't like the time between lunch and tea, when the sun is brightest.'

On the last night, in his raving, he contradicted himself at every turn, He would shriek, 'A man must live without sex.'

And again, 'I have a wife in Poland.'

And then, 'I am not married.'

I remembered how, when he first came, he had told us there were devils at Garthwen, but that he was not afraid of evil spirits. On his first evening in our house, he had shut each door carefully after him (keeping out the devils?). Perhaps, his very reason for coming to the island was because he thought the sea would keep him safe from the pursuing powers of evil.

It may have been a clue to hysteria, to his schizophrenia, the remark he let fall in conversation on his first Christmas here.

'A Russian tickled my throat with a knife, ha! ha!'

I remembered too, how some time before, he had given away all his laying pullets on one pretext or another; one, he had thrown over the wall to a passing dog, muttering:

'The dog can have it. The hen has a devil in its body.' Had he already given himself up to self-flagellation two years before? Was he already beating his breast two Christmases back? He had asked us then to take him with us when we went to the mainland as he wanted to see a doctor. He had complained of pain in his chest and left arm.

42

On a gorse-gold day in the next spring, while he was scything weeds, Cadwaladr had a cerebral thrombosis which left him paralysed down the right side of his body.

He who had for so long been the tormentor, suddenly became the victim of the tormented.

Siani was growing up; she had known no tenderness from her mother, and her father had never relented in his persecution of her, so that she had become a kind of freak, abnormally strong and muscular, with a coarse dark blood-suffused face and a gruff voice. She wore the cast-off clothing of her father and mother, and heavy hobbed boots. As she had grown, so she had become lazier; the one aim of her life was to escape work.

Finding herself mistress of Cadwaladr's befogged existence, she quite openly gloated and whistled as she went about the fields. In front of her father she was still inhibited; though he could not touch her now, she still kept a wary distance between herself and him.

Tudur was more affected by Cadwaladr's overthrow. For one thing, he had never been so cruelly treated as Siani, and the new order, though it brought a revolution into his life, depressed his gay spirits; until at last, he began to enjoy being master of his father's boat, and learned to savour the freedom of independent sea-crossings and fishing with his own lobster pots.

Cadwaladr would sit the whole day long in the house-door, almost motionless. Whereas before, he had worn his cap as a shield to the eyes, now he went hatless, his fine silky hair blowing around his brow; he seemed to have forgotten the necessity for guarding his passing thoughts. Since his mouth was vacant and he never spoke, who could tell if he had any thoughts?

At times, he would writhe his head and clench the fingers of his left hand, as though he suffered a violent spasm of guilt or an uncontrollable rage.

Siani and Tudur, presuming that since their father did not articulate, he could not hear, discussed the future in front of him.

Tudur would laugh, screwing up his eyes and showing a mouthful of strong teeth, saying:

'When the old man goes, then we'll have some fun. I'll buy a big boat for fishing, a really big one; and I'll get rich, selling lobsters. We'll try to get a gramophone and plenty of records, and we'll have a party every week.'

Siani would laugh raucously at her brother's plans, but make no comment. She was thoughtless as an animal, not even aware of her own crude health; but dimly conscious that the hulk of her father had lost its power.

43

For almost the first time in his life, Tudur was now at last free to come and go as he pleased; to visit neighbours without fear of his father suddenly appearing at the door to drive him home at the point of a stick.

He had not long started to take an interest in women; he began to correspond with girls who had visited the island. Wishing to share this pleasure, he would arrive at the house to read one of his secret and treasured love-letters. Spreading himself out in a chair, he would begin to read slowly, his tongue tripping over the complex 'book-learning' language; he read half-aloud, with an air of amused importance, shaking ash from an illicit cigarette through the open window.

On one such occasion, having been made dizzy by a letter and by the prospect of eating a rabbit pie just taken from the oven, he began to recount the fabulous battle of beasts he had come upon one day at sea.

'I'm telling you; there were these two enormous whales, and they were fighting in the middle of the Sound.'

'What colour were they?'

'One was white; the other was a kind of grey like stone. At first, they were going along fast under the skin of the water, and the travelling of their bodies was like a huge swell rolling in the tide-way. Their heads came up out of the sea, and they began to fight, with terrible threshing and blowing.'

'You say there was a great white whale?'

'Ay, sure; it was white, white; and that was the stronger of the two beasts; though the grey one was a stout fighter, too.'

I looked at him, not crediting; yet forced to believe, for his words were created truth. It was no lie he was telling me, but authentic legend; probably an embroidered tale he had learned and had forgotten having learned in childhood; something that in the swagger and elatedness aroused by having had a letter from a girl, had caused him to tell it as a relief for emotion.

But this tale was purest Melville; the great white whale himself, Ahab's Moby Dick had risen in this lad's fantasies. I knew that Tudur had never heard the name of Herman Melville or of Moby Dick.

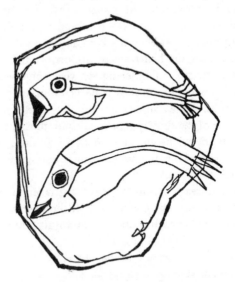

44

In the whole time we have passed on the island, the longest period for which we have been cut off by bad weather was five weeks in midwinter, from the end of November 1950 to the beginning of the New Year 1951.

The last crossing we made before this long isolation was the worst any of us could remember up to that time, and I have experienced nothing like it since.

There was a gale imminent from the sou'west when the boat manned by Jacob and Paul set out for the mainland to fetch me home from a holiday in London.

I was late in reaching the village; the wind was rising so fast that the men could wait no longer. I arrived breathless from running, on the edge of the water at the cove, to see the boat slipping away round the corner of the rocks. Forgetting that I was still wearing city shoes, I ran into the surf, screaming their names. At the last possible moment, Paul turned his head and saw me.

Loosing the painter of the dinghy, he rowed swiftly shorewards; ordered me to jump aboard and to row for dear life, while he held down the stern of the light boat and sought to keep her head into the breakers.

Somehow, we got out of the grinding rocks and the breakers; I scrambled overside the motor boat, and Paul wrapped me in his immense duffle coat, which becoming almost at once soaked with briny spray, prevented my turning my head during the whole night-mare crossing; being seated amidships and in front of the men, I had no means of knowing whether they were still aboard, except once when I heard above the clamour of wind and hissing water Jacob shout warningly to my husband that he must draw the painter of the dinghy more closely in to the stern of the motor boat; for, with the height and depth of a wave, between, the plucking backward of the dinghy was almost enough to tear out the thwart on which they were sitting.

Such a sea was running that I was taken far away beyond the mere fear of drowning; that we should be overwhelmed and sunk at any moment seemed too obvious. Strangely, inky phrases began to press upon one another in my numbed mind.

'Whole seas went over her decks.'

Literary tags came to mind.

'Green seas poured over her hatches, tearing out the strongly battened-down covers.'

Eyes were so blinded by salt that I dared no longer wipe them; salt and water filled the nostrils and trickled down the back of the throat. Whole waves broke on my head and ran, first ice-cold, then warmer as the body's temperature tempered them, on to the ribs and belly and thighs and so away on to the swilled decking.

By mid-Sound, the wind was hysterical. Though we had no mast or stays or sails, not even a bare pole to defy the gale, it was as if the wind screamed against a stern resistance overhead. Over and over again, there ran senselessly through my head the phrase:

'How the wind would whistle through the rigging if we had any rigging for the wind to whistle through.'

The waves were now so monstrous-high, we lost sight of the tall island; the liquid ranges were our whole landskip.

Seas washed from port to starboard across the boat's waist. At those moments of extreme hazard, I would look down at my hand clenched to the gunwale, to see hand and gunwale go down green into the sea, punished by the weight of water; and felt surprise when dripping arm and wood rose again buoyantly high into the air on the crest of the conquered swell.

Never before had the Cafn seemed so true a haven as when, the last danger passed—the rollers at Pen Clogwyn had tried at the last to break us within sight of home—we glided in unbelievable calmness and simplicity over the untroubled water of the anchorage.

The island was a core of silence at the heart of thundering surf that surrounded it on every side. Reaching home, carrying the smell of storm with us, we peeled off trousers and smocks and left them where they fell. Paul stood at the back door to empty water and pebbles out of his sea-boots. He said: 'Two nights ago, there was a terrible stench of bad drains at the back door, so I knew the rotting weed was beginning to roll in with the swell. With such a certain sign of storm coming, I never thought we should be able to come for you.'

After supper, Paul sat half-asleep at the table, relaxed from the hours spent on the sea.

There had been no time to bring any supplies with me; even my dressing-case had been left behind in the crisis.

The islanders had been caught out; we began our five weeks' isolation without the ordinary stocks of supplies normally hoarded at this time of year. It would be impossible to starve on the island save deliberately, for there is so much stock, besides hens and ducks and geese; eggs, butter, milk, vegetables; but there is a monotony in eating rabbit however succulent. Semolina pudding is unexciting. The greatest treat we had at that time was the occasional rock-fish caught in sheltered bays and deeps off the side of the island. It tastes best during the winter months; it should be cooked crisply in deep fat and covered in parsley sauce dashed with wine vinegar.

That night, there was a display of Northern Lights, passionate curtains of red and white fire, a sure sign of tempest. Next day, the barograph at the lighthouse plunged downward.

Flocks of starlings swept into the fields, power-diving the island from the north, making a noise like hundreds of yards of calico being torn apart. Hail broke white: massive thunderclaps burst over the mountain. A lugubrious raven passed slowly, head into the wind, croaking DOOM ON ALL YOUR HOUSES! We were filled as it were

for the first time with the horror of winter's darkest days and nights, and looked forward yearningly to January and the first full moon of the New Year. It was necessary to strain patience and fortitude to the utmost and say, 'Even the worst weather ends sometime.'

There was a spectacular storm: hail and thunder and darkness at noon, succeeded by blue sea and sky towards Ireland. The house-windows reflected a sudden wash of light, the panes taking on the opacity of blind eyes. The solitude had a ghostly quality. Other people are necessary to us, if only to convince us of our own reality.

One evening, as we were walking the west side before sundown, we found one of the inlets was filled with driftwood. A place of slimy clay and treachery, it was easy to get down, but we had to come up again on hands and knees, soaking wet to the thighs, pushing and throwing the wood ahead of us. Among the flotsam was the broad broken-off blade of an oar, like the long oars the old people had left on the beams in the boathouse. It was another wild day's end, and I wondered what was happening out in the world.

The essentials began to give out; flour and sugar, tea and coffee, and for the men, tobacco.

At night, we visited one another, to make careful enquiries about the state of the other's larder.

'Candles is it, you want? Yes, we have candles. You don't have some margarine in exchange, by chance?'

So, we bartered after dark, returning with the precious box of matches, the handful of raisins, the screw of tobacco.

It becomes demoralising after some weeks, to be unable to walk upright, to be forced down almost into the animal posture, forced to lean into the wind; not only is the body buffeted, but the mind also.

Preoccupied with the grim struggle of fending for the next day, we went to bed early to save lamp-oil, and we lay awake praying for a lull in the tempest. The first waking thought was of food. Must I bake today? In what new way could I present a rabbit? Had the spate of water destroyed the watercress in the stream?

'If only the gale would reach hurricane force,' we used to say, at that time. 'If only the gale would blow the buildings away, so that we could be taken off the island. If only there could be an end.'

Birds, herring-gulls and black-backs, oystercatchers and turnstones, stood motionless in the fields. The bays were smothered in thick creamy froth and the long beach under the lighthouse was a heaving mass of discoloured foam like fleece from which the wind whipped tufts and gobs. Jacob's geese were in the habit of standing at the south end, gazing in the direction of South America.

One evening, Tudur visited us secretly after his father was in bed on the clothes chest. I asked him if he could not possibly kill a lamb and let us have part of it. At first he looked doubtful, then he grinned widely, saying, 'Ay, but you mustn't let anyone know about it. I'll do it tomorrow and bring it down about ten o'clock. Don't go to bed, remember.'

The next night, under a starless heaven, he came to the back door with a leg of lamb hidden between two sheets of cardboard, and the horned head wrapped in newsprint. Although it was late, I decided to cook the leg to which grey tufts of wool still clung. At midnight, we feasted on roast meat, and felt that our stomachs were satisfied for the first time in days. As food for the dog, the head was cooked next morning in the largest pot, from which it stared out, with the lid balanced across its horns. By this time, the house was sweet with the smell of real cooking, and I was afraid lest anyone pick up the fragrance on the wind. At midmorning, Merfyn called in. Though he must have been aware of the odour of fresh meat, he made no remark as he sat in his usual place behind the kitchen door, with pale freckled hands clutching the cloth bag.

45

As the bleak, storm-ridden days of darkness went slowly by, the spirit of life slowed until the women were reduced for gossip to what came to be known among us as 'Mouse-talk'; quite literally, we were debased to comparing notes on the mouse-life in our houses.

Christmas came and went; fires smoked sullenly. No greetings cards decorated the mantelshelves, but we made a crib in a corner of the study, and constructed a tree out of twigs from the tamarisk. We found a few sprigs of berried holly behind the chapel.

To crown everything, a thistle seed went into my right eye, and nearly maddened me for days. With a bandaged eye from which water ran freely, I struggled to finish a large canvas in the dreary half-light filtering through the salt-crusted windows.

The New Year days of 1951 came and went; we lost count of time, we felt stranded and forgotten. The radio batteries having given out, we had no knowledge of what the world was saying; we did not know that our plight was being headlined on the radio and in the daily press. Nobody thought of the simple expedient of dropping supplies from the air, or of sending a lifeboat.

By this time, the position had become serious. Not only were our basic supplies almost at an end, but cattle foodstuffs were urgently needed.

Suddenly, one morning, a lighthouse man came to us with wonderful news. A lifeboat was being taken from one station to another along the coast, which necessitated passing through the Sound; the coxwain had offered to pick up provisions for us from the mainland village, if men of the village would co-operate in getting the food down to the Porth Ancr beach.

Wild with relief, we kept watch on the mountain for the lifeboat. As soon as she was sighted, Paul ran from house to house to warn the men. A dinghy was launched and rowed out into the bay to go alongside the lifeboat for the transference of food boxes. At the end of those long dreary five weeks, we saw, out there in the sea, other men. Food boxes were flung aboard the dinghy, and last of all, my leather suitcase.

Rhiannon and I stood at the compass stones at the end of the Cafn, snuffling with emotion, and waving handkerchiefs in thanks to our deliverers.

Our reaction to the food was strange and unexpected. Besides the common staples of life, my mother had sent a basket of exotic delicatessen foodstuffs. These, we spread out over the table, to gloat over. After careful examination, and a close reading of labels, they were put away in the cupboard. We had gone for so long on an austere diet, that we were unprepared for richer fare. It was some days before we had the desire to open the gift-food.

So we celebrated Christmas sometime in January when the gorse bushes were already ablaze with gold; putting out our greeting cards at about the time when we should have been taking them down.

46

In such fashion, I live like Andromeda bound to the rock rude; often writhing to free myself yet cherishing my bonds; at extremest tension, hoping for the wind to blow everything away, so that problems might be solved by elemental means beyond human control.

Through poverty, heartbreak, and drama, it remains the alighting-place of my heart. the point of seeing with a clear eye and mind; a solitary place but blessed by the sun. The life which at first seemed so confining, so stifling, has become the releasing spring, until at last, there is no question of identity.

At the beginning, I prayed:

'Old sea, refresh our hearts.'

The prayer has been answered, over and over again.

Since early summer of this year 1960, a spider has lived on my rosary which hangs beside the hearth; a spider, weaving a web of strong white threads from stone to stone; a source of wonderment to my friends. The homely creature is a cure for superstition, teaching philosophy—for it is constantly there.

'Sorrow in the morning.

Boredom at midday.

A gift in the afternoon.

Hope at night.'

47

As I have already said in recounting the legend of a saint, if only there was a tongue still vocal in the dust; a quiet tongue to speak of promise and fulfilment, but not of blind despairs. From grey crumbs of mortar, what message has come to us, more than ghostly half-understood prayers for admittance to the comfort of our hearths?

Up north from the house, the ruin whose wall sprouts a surrealist face, still binds the island together. The stones that remain have become almost humanised from the touch of hands in many centuries. The ruin gives, like everything else on this deluding scrap

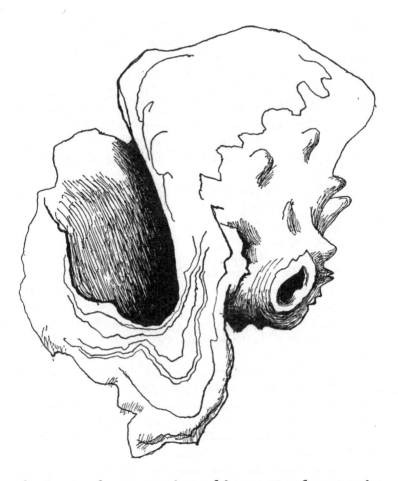

of rock and turf, provocative hints of the past. How fitting it is that the sanctified walls should have crumbled and been torn away, until only an evil face glares out, a harsh mask against the mountain-side which cannot preserve innocence under the vigilant quartering of hawks.

The fragment (and though only a fragment, it seems to have the stubborn lasting quality of the cliffs) sees men love and hate and pass away; binding us as surely as itself is bound, into the myth that Time repeats with small variations through the years. In its haunted shell it enshrines and raises up the essence of legions of dead, innocent men and sinners who have lived here. Countless souls have perished for every stone that has crumbled from the pile.

Altar, transept, nave, and apse, like martyr's breath, all vanished! But just as there rises from the few remaining walls, a stern emanation of the highest possible upward-straining of the human spirit, so also does there rise as if from living choristers, a plain-chant from perished throats. They fill the house with their singing, but they are more than voicers of canticles, for in their disembodied state is lostness and yearning as if they felt too keenly the cold austerity of outer regions of space.

We live on top of a graveyard of long-boned men. Deserted even by the worms, they bide their time in the earth, ochre-stained from their sojourn there, grinning like the dogfish in the Sound.

Cadwaladr and Nans and their children; Merfyn; the drowned oysterfishers; the melancholy old woman who went over the cliff with only birds for witnesses; Sarah, Twm, Dai Penmon; Jacob and Rhiannon and their lovely daughter Eira with youth dizzy and triumphant; the drunken engineer; unhappy Stewart and Alice; and Friedrich who first led me here, and was himself disillusioned; Paul and I; we are all in the danse macabre, the fatal play of life and death.

The stained bones underground feel our dancing measure. The brisk feet leap over our own future grave-plots.

A little larger than life, dancing with more abandon and grotesqueness than the others; with the devil nudging his elbow and manipulating a wire in his head, is Caliban the beast; the native genius of Prospero's island; of mine; of any island.

On this small stage, this microcosm, in the middle of a scene, the shadow of death falls on the players.

1946–1960

Afterword

Bardsey Island (or Ynys Enlli under its lovelier, more alliterative Welsh form) rises out of the western sea off Braich-y-pwll like a hump-backed whale. From the mainland it deceives, concealing its gentler western slopes behind its mountain. Only two miles separate the northern tip of the island from Lleyn, but the voyage out is more like six miles, from the village of Aberdaron, round the point of Pen-y-cil, then over the treacherous waters of the Sound, round the southern tip of Bardsey to a landing near the lighthouse. When the tide is running, the Sound is a maelstrom of thrashing waters vying for room in the narrows. Brenda Chamberlain, following Homer, describes these waters as 'wine-dark', and nothing could be more apt, for so swiftly and darkly does the tide run that often opposing floods run counter with a wall a foot high between them'.

Colonel Colby's first Ordance Survey map published in 1839 shows the island's topography much as it is today. There along the single lane with old houses either side, life has passed immemorially. Who knows what prehistoric people sought refuge here? The early saints, dipping their weary feet in holy wells all along the spine of the Lleyn peninsula, arrived, lived out their ascetic lives and laid their bones here. But mostly the island bears the stamp of the 'old people' of the last century, surviving into this one: "men of faded photographs; bearded, in Tam o'Shanters, taller than men are now; more heroic, removed from the present into saga-land by the passage of time".

Then followed mainland curiosity in the years just before the war. Most of the old folk departed, like some disturbed wild species, leaving the island and most of its houses to the birds, rabbits, seals and the lighthouse keepers. Mainlanders came bringing their various neuroses; Stewart Hopkinson and his half-estranged wife who hated the island and threatened to leave any day. And Brenda Chamberlain.

The impact of meeting those already there, still with that lacing of 'old folk', affected her deeply. "The suave, secretive faces of seafarers, with the mouths of men who have *almost* mastered fear" (my italics). That is indicative, for Brenda came to the island part-wounded in some way, came like a pilgrim searching out healing, hoping *almost* to master fear. One's first impression of Brenda was of vulnerability. She was small, yet strong of bone with a tall, gothic countenance. But she was susceptible to deep hurt, which she held within. To seek an island is the wish of those who suffer too deeply from the cut and thrust of mainland life.

She took to the island at once, yet was half-afraid, under no illusions as to its insidious cruelties. "Puppet strings took me by the hair roots, drawing me back to the house in the quiet dusk". Her pessimism shows through, yet it is a poetic pessimism, reminiscent of Rilke — "a bird power-dived. Alas, humankind; featherless, wingless, crawling the earth". But she roots down and very soon in *Tide-race* appears the passage where she watches the seals basking and fishing, taking on the aspect of myth. "Below us, a seal cow lay on her back in the bottle-green gloom of the cavern... Come to me, come to me. Her arms extended, folded again to her creamy underside. So great was the human mermaid attraction that I could have leapt to my death by drowning... A woman on land and a silkie in the sea".

In many ways, Bardsey was ideal for Brenda. It was not that she needed a new landscape to spark off some inspired seam of painting, as Pembrokeshire sparked off Graham Sutherland. She was not simply painter, but writer, poet. She did not really *need* people or landscape, she simply needed to confront them, explore them as a blind child explores a new face with its fingers, sometimes as sadly, to see how far she could get with them. She records, she does not comment much, yet in recording brings out the poetry of place. "If I had a thousand years in which to learn the secrets of the sea, the force of my desire would become lost in the thought of eternity. Though tomorrow may be nothing to me: I nothing to tomorrow, today is mine."

She would call at our house, out of the blue, her timing controlled more by tide than by clock, with her tall, handsome, monosyllabic Paul, would enter the small world of our children, then depart just as abruptly, as though called back to the island. "You who are in the safety of the world, can you guess what this going home means to the islander?" You felt she would be your friend for life, but would never need you. Yet how wrong that was, as those of us who did not discern her need in the last years came to know only too well. For even as she cried, it sounded like poetry, childlike, keening, yet with that sharp ear for the wind's whispers and the rustle of adder in the hedge bank.

As she sang her songs of innocence, there was a great deal of experience to her too, perhaps more than she needed. She was a Bangor girl, educated there, and she followed her artistic bent by attendance at the Royal Academy Schools where she met, and subsequently married John Petts, the painter, engraver and typographer. Together they settled at Llanllechid in the hills behind Bangor, at the beginning of the war, where they produced the inimitable Caseg Broadsheets, a pattern for that mixture of word and image beloved of the Welsh. For though some claim the Welsh are visually blind, a reading of Welsh poetry soon corrects this assumption.

Ac yna trwy egni'r gaeaf,
Arwyddion goruchafiaeth yr haf —
Gwynion bach, gwyrddion bach
O'r pridd du...

writes Gwyn Thomas

And then through Winter's force
Come signs of summer's conquest
Little whites, little greens
Out of the black earth...

Such images from nature, her colours, sights, sounds, a fox traversing the mountain top, blazing red against the setting sun, the sheer profligacy of nature...

The green vibrancy worn yellow
with its prophecies red and black...
(Euros Bowen)

All this is abundant in Welsh poetry from the beginning, for do not the Welsh in their green landscape live within touch of heaven? Brenda early found her vocation as poet, whether in prose, verse, painting or drawing. The story of the Gwasg y Gaseg enterprise is told in *Alun Lewis and the Making of the Caseg Broadsheets*. Those broadsheets are now precious collectors' items.

But alas, the sunderings of war. John was torn away on national service, joining 224 Parachute Field Ambulance, where I met him, serving in Europe and the Middle East. Their parting broke the bond. They separated. She was in Germany soon after its defeat, staying with Karl von Laer, to whom she dedicated her first volume of verse, *The Green Heart*.

It was in Shinwell's hard winter of 1947 that she settled in Bardsey with Paul, and stayed till 1961, with occasional sorties to the mainland, arranging framing for an exhibition at Gimpel Fils in London, or printing, or simply feeling her feet on the mainland, testing out friends, who was still faithful to life's poetry, who betrayed by the daily treadmill.

I recall even printing one of her broadsheets myself, though I have no trace of it. No, she was not short on experience, if one means the prints life lays upon the heart in its passage. Yet always she was shot through with innocence. Even when Paul and she seemed to drift apart and Enlli possibly soured (who is to know?), she sought another island amidst the wine-dark sea. Once, when my wife and I sailed out of Piraeus in the little island steamer, I stopped off at Aegina to pay homage to the temple of Aphaea while my wife sailed on to Ydra off the tip of the Pelopennessos. Mistaking her for English, the skipper declared for her benefit: "There is Englishman at top of hill". And sure enough, when Judith climbed the hill, there behind lemon-yellow curtains and a jar of golden asphodel was Brenda.

But there is no doubt the centre of her 59 years on this earth were those at Ynys Enlli and *Tide-race* is their monument. From the island she sang her poetry like a syren, tempting the unwary to brave the treachery of the waters and share in her troubled and precarious ecstasy. She soaked up the island and its moods, its volatile weather, the tide-race in the Sound, rippling black silk beneath the shadow of the mountain, the cry of shearwater, the dip and dart of oyster-catchers, the basking mermaid-life of seals, but above all the in-grown living of the islanders, the shooting of a sick cow for want of the vet and where to bury it ("Wasn't sure where the other buggers had been buried" moans Cadwaladr), strange nostrums for sick children, the guarded relationships of spouses, the intermittent mourning for the mainland that would offer them no great solace should they fall for its temptations. For the islanders too have their neuroses, the women in their perpetual insecurity, the men at sea in a storm, no doctor within reach should a child fall mysteriously ill; Cadwaladr haunted by a dead neighbour: "Old Dai tried to grab me last night, and there was a man in the tower last week, singing to himself about a shipwreck".

Tide-race is the record of an inner voyage, embellished by drawings of what her eye caught. There is nothing quite like it. Although Brenda was a very successful painter, with several one-man shows in London and her works placed in most Welsh collections and elsewhere, *Tide-race* is her true memorial, her benefaction to us who dwell on the mainland and ponder sometimes as we look over the Sound.

Jonah Jones